Enjoy Healing Now

Jesus, EFT & Me

Donna Crow

Enjoy Healing Now: Jesus, EFT & Me by Donna Crow

Books may be purchased by contacting the publisher and author at:

Cover Design: Donna Crow
Interior Design: Donna Crow
Publisher: Donna Crow

First Paperback Edition 2014
First EBook Edition 2006
Printed in USA

www.donnacrow.com
www.fol-hs.com
www.enjoyhealingnow.com

Dear Reader:

In 2006, I was supernaturally healed of a seemingly incurable illness. Immediately upon hearing my good news, people who knew me via the Internet were eager to hear what had happened and perhaps glean some puzzle piece from my experience that might help them to enjoy healing themselves. In response to their queries, I created an Internet discussion group where I shared my experience and the knowledge it was based on.

After I posted about five messages to the group, a number of members contacted me to say my messages were looking like chapters in a book. They enthusiastically requested that I put them together in book form, which I did. What you have in your hands is the end product, and I believe you will find it filled with powerful, useable information.

The information I share is unique and includes Christian EFT methods, as well as the specific Biblical truth I acted on, which resulted in my instant healing. I am not unique in my ability to hear and act on truth and, as a result, receive help from Heaven. I believe anyone can do so and *Enjoy Healing Now* in the privacy of their own home, just as I did.

For those who do not know my background, or me I will share a brief health biography.

In the summer of 1988, when I was 38 years old, I went from a little fatigued, but generally healthy, to profoundly ill. The doctors who saw me could not diagnose the problem. Since they were not able to determine exactly what was wrong, they could provide no treatment options. I had to go home and figure out how to stay alive on my own.

After several months of fighting to live, I finally turned a corner and seemed to be improving. Nevertheless, I remained mostly bedfast and completely housebound for several years after that. It was a long, slow journey of gradual recovery. After much personal research, I came to understand that I didn't actually have a "disease". What I had was an overall breakdown of my health, which started with Mercury fillings and ended with adrenal fatigue, leaky gut syndrome, gluten intolerance, and a host of other health challenges that kept me from totally regaining my health through natural means.

As a result of my own research, education, and self-treatment using various natural products and protocols, I did increase in strength and enjoyed hours of "normal" here and there. After eighteen years, however, I still had not reached the point of total recovery. Though I could make short journeys out into the world and could be up and about more often, I still had to conscientiously and carefully guard my health to prevent relapses.

While I was studying natural health, I was also intently studying the Bible regarding healing, and I was praying, praying, praying, and always expecting to be healed. Finally, in February 2006, it happened; I was instantly healed and it was astonishingly wondrous. How amazing it was to possess normal energy instantly. From that day on, I have been active and productive without becoming sick and requiring bed rest to recover.

The following messages share my unique use of EFT to help me connect with God's healing power and receive a miracle. You will find practical instructions, which you can act on in order to take steps toward your own healing. Truth is truth for all. The truth that set me free can also set you free.

With joy,
Donna Crow

About EFT

As you read these messages, you will notice I occasionally mention something called "EFT." EFT is an abbreviation for Emotional Freedom Technique and refers to a simple, self-applied acupressure technique, which can be used to eliminate negative emotions produced by our biochemistry. Gary Craig is the one who chose to call it EFT and was instrumental in making it known to a wide audience. Dr. Roger Callahan, however, is the one who actually discovered this acupressure technique, and he did so quite accidentally.

Dr. Callahan was working with a woman who had a serious water phobia when it happened. He had worked with her for about a year and had seemingly made no progress. In one of his sessions with this woman, he asked her to visualize going out to his swimming pool (within her view) and splashing water in her face. As usual, when she tried to imagine doing that, she felt extreme nausea. Dr. Callahan had been studying acupressure and he had recently learned that the acupoint for nausea was under the eye, so he said to her, *"Why don't I just tap on that acupoint for nausea, while you picture splashing water in your face, and see if we can eliminate the nausea."* He tapped for about 30 seconds whereupon she jumped up shouting that it was gone.

Of course, he was happy; assuming she meant the nausea was gone. She, however, was happy because her phobia was gone! She ran out the door to the deep end of the pool and knelt down and began to splash water in her face. He then realized that not only had her nausea gone, but the phobia had also gone with it. It was an astonishing moment, and he wondered if it would work for others with different issues. He tried it with other clients, such as Viet Nam veterans with post-traumatic stress syndrome, and found that tapping on acupressure points worked equally as well with them; more than 80% of the time. Enter Gary Craig, who heard about Dr. Callahan's work and became his student. Gary simplified the technique for the average person to use, named it EFT and began to spread the good news.

Eventually, I became Gary Craig's student. I taught myself EFT using Gary's on-line manual. I used it a little here and there, but really didn't understand exactly how to incorporate it into my life until one of

a

my brothers died. I was devastated. My mother had died not long before, and I was still grieving her loss when my brother died. Donna, the normally strong person who supported everyone else, sank like a rock. I felt such grief, and nausea, and fatigue that it was scary. I considered calling a friend, but I felt like, "If I have to say out loud that my brother died, I will die of grief." So, I prayed. I said, "Lord, I'm not doing well here; I need help. I feel scary sad, and I don't feel like I can call anyone. Please help me."

Instantly, I remembered EFT. Fortunately, I remembered how to do it, and believed it was a clear answer from the Lord, so I immediately applied it. It took me less than two minutes to tap the specific acupressure points, while focusing on what I was feeling. By the time I finished, I felt totally normal. All the sadness, grief, nausea and fatigue lifted, and I felt normal. I was still of the mind that I wished my brother was alive, but I didn't feel devastated that he was gone. It was a shocking and wonderful moment.

I immediately began to voraciously study EFT, and became an EFT coach, receiving certificates in both Basic and Advanced EFT. I have used this technique to help me to eliminate emotions that conflicted with my faith regarding healing. What I began to realize is that I believed one thing and felt another. With EFT, I was able to eliminate those lying emotions that conflicted with my faith.

I don't give basic instructions on EFT in these messages because I am talking to people who were already familiar with EFT and how to do it. It is a simple technique of tapping on acupressure points while focusing on negative emotions or physical symptoms. It is easy to do and works more than 80% of the time.

For free basic instructions go to:

http://www.fol-hs.com

EFT is part of my story, and that is why I have shared about it here. You do not, however, need to know how to do EFT to receive healing from the Lord or to benefit from these messages.

For further information:
http://www.fol-hs.com
http://www.enjoyhealingnow.com

b

a

EFT Simplified Instructions

Read all the way through before starting.

First

While massaging the tender point, repeat this phrase 3 times:

Even though I (fill in the blank) I deeply and completely love and accept myself.

Fill in the blank with your issue. Ex: *'I'm afraid of spiders.'*

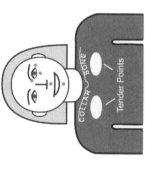

© 2010 Donna Crow

Tender Points

COLLAR BONE

The tender points are located on the flat area of the upper chest. See white ovals in graphic above.

NOTE: You can tap on either side of your face, or you can tap on both sides.

Second

Reduce your phrase to just your issue: Ex: *I'm afraid of spiders."*

Now, starting at the eyebrow point (either one) say your reduced phrase and tap on that point 5-7 times. Repeat this at each point until you have tapped on all 8 pressure points. 5 on face, 1 oncollar bone, 1 under arm and side of the hand. 8 in total. Repeat on all pressure points.

This should not take more than a minute or two to finish.

Important

Use the **TIP** of your index finger to **TAP** on the points. **DO NOT** use the **FLAT** of your index finger to **PAT**.

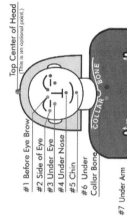

Top Center of Head
(This is an optional point.)

#1 Before Eye Brow
#2 Side of Eye
#3 Under Eye
#4 Under Nose
#5 Chin
#6 Under Collar Bone
#7 Under Arm
4" Below Armpit

COLLAR BONE

© 2010 Donna Crow

NOTE: Use all the finger tips of one hand to tap on the Karate Chop points of your other hand.

© 2010 Donna Crow

#8 Karate Chop Points

You can also tap on the center of the top of your head, if you desire. Some find this point unpleasant to tap on, other really like it.

CONGRATULATIONS! You have completed one "round" of EFT.

If the issue is not resolved, do a few more rounds until you feel free of the offending issue.

This is a very simplified demonstration, meant to remind you how to do the process. Stubborn issues might require more tapping, or even coaching.

For effective and experience EFT coaching, email:
Donna@DonnaCrow.com

Table of Contents

Message One

I AM Willing

And when He had come down from the mountain, great multitudes followed Him.

And behold, a leper came to Him and bowed down to Him, saying, "Lord, if You are willing, You can make me clean."

And He stretched out His hand and touched him saying,

"I am willing; be cleansed."

And immediately his leprosy was cleansed.

Do you want to know what God is like?

Look at Jesus.

Do you want to know what God's will is?

Look at Jesus.

Do you want to know if God wants you well?

Look at Jesus.

In John 8:9, Jesus said,

"If you have seen Me, you have seen the Father."

*I*f Jesus stood in front of you right now and you said to Him, "Lord, if you are willing, you can heal me," do you think He would reply differently to you than He did to the leper?

1

I don't.

I think He would say to you,

> "I am willing, be healed."

If you want to know if God wants you well, look at Jesus Who said,

> "I am willing"

Message Two

One Can't Believe
The Impossible

"One can't believe the impossible,"
said Alice.

"I daresay you haven't had much practice,"
said the Queen.

"When I was your age I always
did it for half an hour a day."

"Why sometimes I've believed as many
as six impossible things before breakfast."

*I*f you are looking for teaching that will back up your current situation of ill health, these messages may not be of interest to you.

If you are looking for teaching, backed by the Word, that says your situation can change, then you are in the right place. Here you will hear that, according to the Word, Jesus Christ is the same yesterday, today, and forever.

According to the Word, Jesus healed all who came to Him.

It is logical to conclude that if Jesus is the same yesterday, today, and forever, and He healed all who came to Him yesterday, then He heals all who come to Him today, and will heal all who come to Him tomorrow.

Now I know the very first thing most people will think is, "But He doesn't! Many people pray and ask to be healed, and they don't get healed!"

Well, I would encourage you right up front to make a choice. You can put your confidence in your experience and that of others, which conflicts with the Word, or you can put your confidence in the Word, which says you can change your experience.

For now,
just let it be okay that you don't fully understand
why some people don't get healed.

Just let it be okay that the lack is probably
on the part of the person, and not God.

Just let it be okay that, that doesn't mean
they are a bad person, or spiritually inferior.

Just let it be okay that we all see through a glass darkly,
that none of us sees with perfect clarity.

Let your heart be a judgment-free zone.

Do not judge yourself for not being well.

Do not judge others for not being well.

Just let it be okay to be where you are now.

And let it be okay to get well,
even if someone else did not.

I repeat . . .
Let your heart be a judgment free zone.

Don't be afraid to have faith.

Don't be afraid to believe the impossible.

"All things are possible to the one who believes."

4

-Jesus Christ

Are you afraid you won't be able to believe? Are you afraid you don't have enough faith? Consider this:

> "Without faith it is impossible to please God for the one who comes to Him must believe that He is and that He is a rewarder of those who diligently seek Him."
> —Paul

Okay. So it's impossible to please God without faith. Do you think God would require something of you that you cannot give? He does not!

You are a being of faith, hope, and love. Deep in your heart you know sickness is wrong. Faith is woven into who you are as a New Creation in Christ.

You *can* live in faith and please God.

Faith does not offend God.
Faith pleases God.

"All things are possible to the one who believes,"
said Jesus.

"One can't believe the impossible,"
said Alice.

Consider the Queen's reply to Alice:

"I dare say you haven't had much
practice," said the Queen.

"When I was your age I always did it for
half an hour a day."

"Why sometimes I've believed as many
as six impossible things before
breakfast."

"All things are possible to the one who believes,"

said Jesus.

"Without faith it is impossible to please God,"
said Paul.

Believing the impossible pleases God. Without believing the impossible you cannot please God.

"The things impossible with men are possible with God,"
said Jesus.

Believing the impossible is believing God. Jesus told people over and over again,

"Your faith has healed you."

Your faith can heal YOU, and it will please God.

Let me ask you this: If Jesus came right now and stood in your room where you are and said to you,

"Be healed,"

How would you feel in your heart? How would you respond? Would you jump up with joy and enthusiasm, knowing it was a done deal?

I suspect the answer is, "Yes."

Why?

Because His willingness would be obvious to you. You would be unable to deny Him or His willingness. You would joyfully accept healing with childlike faith.

Do you really think that if Jesus came and stood in front of you right now and you asked Him to heal you that He would say "No"?

The truth is that Jesus is there right now—just as real and just as willing—saying, "Be healed." He is just as willing for you to be healed as He was willing for others to be healed who came to Him 2000 years ago.

6

My goal here is to speak the Word so you can see this with eyes of faith, and receive your healing. Faith comes by hearing the Word. Your faith is what will make you whole, and the Word is what feeds your faith. So, I plan to share the Word that fed my faith, in hopes that it will feed yours also.

It took me 18 years to figure this out. Well, actually I prayed wrong for 18 years, then I finally figured out what I was doing wrong, and prayed correctly, then I was healed.

"You're faith has made you well,"
said Jesus.

"Without faith it is impossible to please God,"
said Paul.

"One can't believe the impossible,"
said Alice.

"All things are possible to the one who believes,"
said Jesus.

"I daresay you haven't had much practice,"
said the Queen.

Which voice do you want to listen to?

Starting today:

Practice believing the impossible.

Starting today:

Practice believing Jesus Christ is the same,
"Yesterday, today and forever."

Starting today;

Practice believing that Jesus heals all who come to Him today,
just like He did yesterday.

Just let it be okay that you don't

understand why some aren't healed.

Just let it be okay
that you believe you can be healed,
even if some haven't been healed.

Just let it be okay that you don't understand.

Just let it be okay that you believe God
and you please Him.

Message Three

Your Faith
Has Made You Well
Part 1

"Your faith has made you well,"
said Jesus.

"Faith is the substance of things hoped for,
the evidence of things not seen,"
said Paul.

Faith is the substance of the healing you hope for,
the evidence that it is yours, though it is so far unseen.

"Your faith has made you well,"
said Jesus.

"Without faith it is impossible to please God,"
said Paul.

Faith pleases God.

I can hear the enemy causing confusion right now, saying. "Read down further in Hebrews 11. Some people suffered by faith. Read it, it says,

"They were: "tortured . . . they experienced mockings and scourgings, yes also chains and imprisonment.

They were "stoned, they were sawn in two, they were tempted, they were put to death by the sword . . . "

"Faith is not some magic wand you can wave and make bad stuff go away," says the enemy.

It is true that some people, by faith, suffer for Christ and the message of truth.

However. NOWHERE in the list do you see:

By faith, they: were sick,
               were crippled,
               were in constant pain,
               had insomnia,
               had seizures,
               had mental illness,
               had cancer,
               had MS,
               had diabetes,
               had Lyme Disease,
               etc.

Yes, it does take faith to stay faithful to God, and continue to believe in Him and His goodness, and to continue to walk in obedience, when you are sick and in pain. It *does* please God for you to stay faithful in those times. Jesus did say, "In the world you will have tribulation," but nowhere did He call sickness (or pain or disease) **tribulation**, and then ask you to walk it out in faith. He healed *all* who came to Him (of *all* diseases) and said, "Your faith has healed/saved you."

You don't exercise faith to be sick; you exercise faith to be well, and you will not offend God if you decide to believe that He is a God of compassion, Whose mercies never fail. You will not offend Him if you decide to believe He wants you well. You will please Him. Wanting to be well does not mean that you are not willing to suffer for Christ, or that you are spiritually shallow.

Let's just test your doctrine here for a moment. What do you really believe? Use your imagination here and pretend an angel of the Lord has come and is standing next to you and saying,

10

"I'm going to ask you a question in a moment, and you must answer this question correctly. If you do not, it will cost you the life of the person you love most." (Of course this would not happen in real life and is not how God operates. Just go with me here.)

Our imaginary angel continues,

"You only have one chance to answer correctly and you cannot choose to not answer."

Ready? Here is the question:

Is sickness a gift from God to make you more spiritual?

Don't answer yet!

For those of you who are extremely confused (because you have tried to understand truth by looking at other people's experiences or your own experience, instead of looking to the Word as your source of truth), I'll give you a hint.

"If you have seen Me, you have seen the Father,"

—Jesus, in John 8:9

". . . and He (Jesus) went about doing good, and healing ALL those who were oppressed by the devil; (devil = adversary) for God was with Him." —Acts 10:38

Remember:

If you want to know what God is like, look at Jesus.

If you want to know what God's will is, look at Jesus.

Okay, back to the question. (And remember the seriousness of a right answer. Consult your heart, and then answer.)

Is sickness a gift from God to make you more spiritual?

I'm hoping your heart gave a resounding," No!" I'm hoping you know in your heart of hearts that God does not put disease on people to bless them. You know from first-hand experience that disease is emotionally wounding.

You have two choices:

You can believe that God is Who He says He is,

"I am the Lord that heals you."
—Exodus 15:26

Or you can believe God wants you to suffer for your faith by being sick. Just ask your heart which statement gives you peace. Which statement feels right in your heart?

That 'knowing' in your heart is faith. Let your heart rest there. Decide to believe the truth and rest in the knowledge that He is the Lord that heals you.

Jesus is God's will in action.

Jesus is God's will revealed.

Jesus healed ALL who came to Him.

Jesus said,

"Your faith has healed you."

If you agree in your heart that,

He is the Lord that heals you,

(even if you aren't well yet), then you have some faith. For now, just rest in that and ignore the questions.

Today,

Practice believing that He is the Lord that heals you.

You are on the way to having faith that makes you well. Don't try to force it, just rest in it.

Message Four

Your Faith
Has Made You Well
Part 2

"Your faith has made you well,"
said Jesus.

"Faith comes by hearing
and hearing by the Word of God,"
said Paul.

*T*here are many teachings from the Word regarding healing. The good news is that you don't have to know every one of them to get healed. Maybe one will raise your faith. Maybe two. Maybe three. It's kind of like that TV game show, *Wheel of Fortune*, where they have a word puzzle that contestants try to solve, one letter at a time. Some "get it" faster than others.

We also have a puzzle, and we already know the answer:

<u>Your</u> <u>faith</u> <u>has</u> <u>made</u> <u>you</u> <u>well</u>

Even though a person can read the answer, and know it mentally, doesn't mean they *get it* so that it is a reality to them. Even though they have the answer, it can still be a puzzle.

My hope is that as I share one truth at a time, the answer will become a heart reality; so that you *get it;* so it is no longer puzzling to you. Some people will only need a little bit of encouragement; others will need more, but every one of us is wired to *get it.*

Remember to let your heart be a judgment-free zone.

Do not judge yourself for not *getting it*
as quickly as you would like.

Do not judge others who don't seem to be getting it.

It took me 18 years to get it. It seems like it took Hezekiah less than an hour to *get it*. It took Job 8 months. It's all good. I'd rather have been a Hezekiah, but I wasn't. Nevertheless, I am well now.

Relax, and know that each truth I share from the Word will feed your faith. Faith comes by hearing the Word of God. Don't try to force it to grow; that will diminish it. The Holy Spirit is on the inside of you to help you to connect with truth. Don't strive; let Him do the heavy lifting.

You know that it feels right that Jesus healed ALL who came to Him. Enjoy that feeling in your heart and ignore the doubt in your head; just for a while.

That feeling is faith.

Enjoy the feeling you have when you consider that Jesus is God's will in action, and you realize that He healed all who came to Him.

That feeling is faith.

You could experience *getting it* at any time, at any point along the way. For some, the little bit that I have shared will be enough for their faith to rise to the point of being the "substance of the thing hoped for." Others (who are like I was) have more inner obstacles and will require more truth to feed their faith to the point of *getting it*. It's all good.

I plan to keep talking until I have shared all that I know to share on the subject. Perhaps it will be enough for someone here. If not, I encourage you to find someone who has more truth, or a different angle on the truth than I do and, as Jesus taught, "keep on seeking until you find." In the original Greek that statement was written in, it actually says, "keep on asking and you shall receive, keep on seeking and you will find, keep on knocking, and the door will be opened to you."

God guarantees if you seek Him
you will find Him,
if you seek Him with all your heart.

You might need His help to do that; I did. I was so fatigued emotionally that I had to ask Him to help me to seek Him with all my heart. My heart felt like it had Chronic Fatigue Syndrome. I was emotionally tired, but He helped me to seek Him and His truth. If you feel flat emotionally, just be honest with Him and tell Him how you are feeling. He knows anyway, but when you acknowledge your feelings and ask for help, He will be gracious and compassionate, and will respond by supplying what you need.

If you seek with Him all your heart
you will find Him.

If you have seen Jesus,
you have seen the Father.

Jesus is the will of God in action.

Jesus healed ALL who came to Him.

Just enjoy these truths, and your faith will grow.

Message Five

What I Prayed

*O*kay, I'm going to tell you what I prayed. First I want to say that I don't think this is the only way to pray. It is how I prayed, and it did work for me. For me, this was a prayer of faith.

Some people "hold on" and the answer finally comes.

Some people "let go" and they get their breakthrough.

Some people just say, "Lord, please heal me," and it happens.

Others call for the elders and get prayed for, and it happens.

Some people cry and get pitiful, and they "get it."

Some people praise God, and they "get it."

Some people just say, "to heck with it" and give up, and they "get it."

Some people do all the above and are still sick. That would refer to me prior to my recent healing, so I have a couple of points here. My way is not the only way, or even the best way. It is just *my way,* and it will work for some, and not for others. The other point is that if you have done all the above and none of it worked, then perhaps what I did will also work for you, so keep listening.

Before I share what I prayed, I want to say this is not some Christian incantation that you can recite, and bingo-bango, you're well. No eye of newt, Christian white magic here. This prayer is basically a legal declaration.

You see I found that approaching God on an emotional level was not getting the job done for me. I felt (after a lot of study and prayer) that I could get what I wanted if I approached it legally—not legalistically but legally. That just worked for me. When I went to the Word and understood what it meant to be in a Covenant relationship with the Lord, my legal position did evoke positive emotions in me but my confidence was not in those emotions, it was in my legal position. I trusted God to honor His Word.

If you do not understand that, as a believer, you are in a covenant relationship with God, then I would highly recommend a trip to the local bookstore to find some teaching on that. Or perhaps do a Web search. Understanding the legally binding covenant you have with the Lord will greatly strengthen you in your faith.

In a nutshell, a covenant relationship is sort of like being blood brothers or sisters. You mix your blood together, and you swear that whatever you have is theirs and whatever they have is yours, and you sit down and establish the rules of your particular covenant. God did this with us. He basically said, "You do what I want (love Him, believe in His Son as the Savior, listen to His voice and obey Him), and I will do what you want (which is to be spiritually restored, physically healed, provided for, protected, guided, etc.)." My prayer is based on that covenant. I will share more on this after I share my prayer.

Why am I sharing the exact prayer? Well, I have listened to so many teachings on healing that didn't tell me how to receive. They invariably said something like, "Just lift up your hands and receive from the Lord now." Unfortunately, that just didn't work for me, and I kept saying to myself, *"Will someone please tell me how to pray in a way that makes sense to me, and makes me feel like I have done it right?"* I somehow knew that if I prayed right I would be healed, so I pressed in, in an attempt to figure out how to do it myself.

I should note that I had studied and meditated on the scriptures that my prayer was based on and believed them to be true for me, when I prayed this prayer. I also was extremely ticked off. I was certain that healing belonged to me, and I was very angry that the enemy was oppressing me, and I was in the mood to oppress him in a serious way. I had had enough, and I was determined to pray with authority and be healed. I knew my legal standing and, with boldness and a bit of anger, I prayed. I was loud, and spoke in the manner in which you would speak to someone who was abusing an innocent person. I knew I was in the right and didn't have to take sickness anymore.

So here is the prayer that worked for me:

"I thank you, Father, that my sins are forgiven through Jesus,

that I am the righteousness of God in Christ,

that I am a new creation in Christ,

that You have transferred me from the kingdom of darkness to the Kingdom of Light; not because I am perfect, but because I am forgiven.

I thank You that, because my sins are forgiven, I am not under the curse.

Your Word says You have set before me the blessing and the curse, and that we can choose the blessing, and bless ourselves by You.

I know that sickness is a result of the curse, and freedom from sickness is a benefit of the blessing.

By choosing Christ, I have chosen the blessing.

I know that sickness is a result of the curse, and I thank You that Christ became a curse for me, and I am no longer under the curse.

Because Christ has redeemed me from the curse of the law, I am redeemed from sickness, and sickness has no legal right to stay in my body.

I thank you that all the promises of God are YES in Jesus.

That means that I can have anything You promised because Jesus paid the price for me; and my sins are forgiven, and

You are not withholding anything from me, because my sins are forgiven.

Because my sins are forgiven, all the promises are yes for me.

I thank You that healing is a promise of God and that it is YES in Jesus.

I thank You that Jesus heals all who come to Him.

I thank You that Jesus bore my sickness and carried my pain, and by His scourging I am healed.

I believe Jesus is my Savior, not only from sin, but also from the curse of the law, which is sickness.

The Word also says that whatever we ask in Jesus' name, we shall receive. And whatever we pray believing, we shall receive. And if we pray according to Your will, we know that You hear us; and we know that if You hear us, we have what we have asked of You.

Jesus also said that, even if we say to a mountain, *"be removed and cast into the sea,"* it will happen if we have faith and do not doubt.

He also said, all things you ask in prayer believing, you shall receive. Lord, I ask You to honor Your Word, and be my Healer, and take sickness from the midst of me.

I know that Jesus has given me authority over all the power of the enemy. So, Satan, I take authority over you, and in the name of Jesus, I command you to let go of my body. I command any unclean spirit of sickness, or infirmity, to leave my body now! (Shouting).

I say that sickness has no right to stay in my body, and in the name of Jesus, I command sickness to leave my body now! I speak to my body, in the name of Jesus, and I say, be healed, be whole and work perfectly now!

I confess that Jesus is my Healer, and by His stripes I am healed.

I believe I have prayed according to Your Word, and I believe You have heard me, and that I have the thing I have asked for.

By faith, I believe I have received, and I declare that, according to Your Word, I am healed!"

When I finished the last statement, *according to Your Word, I am healed,* the power of God hit me. I repeated it about three times—*according to Your Word I am healed*—and I felt more of God and less of sickness with each statement. I knew it was a done deal.

Truthfully, you don't have to have that much scripture to stand on to get well, but I had been ill for so long that I made sure I had a good case, so to speak. Generally, I simply declare that sickness is illegal because Jesus has redeemed me from sickness (the curse of the law), and I command it to go in His name, and it does. But, at the time that I prayed this prayer, I needed more ammunition for my own faith to activate.

What I Prayed

Message Six

If Your Heart
Does Not Condemn You
Part 1

You have seen the prayer I prayed. Perhaps it makes sense to you; perhaps it does not.

I have so many thoughts swimming in my head, it is hard to know where to start. I guess one thing I can say is that I purposely did not list all the scripture that prayer is based on. I just think it needs to be hunted for and ferreted out. Getting a concordance and finding this information on your own will make it more real to your own heart. It is too easy to get into mental assent and mistake it for faith, when just reading down the line and mentally agreeing. To get the truth into your heart, you need to hunt for it like your life depended on it, with a hungry heart.

Another point along those lines is that I am not under the impression that those reading this are spiritually clueless. I suspect most are Christians, and I believe what John said about you, in 1 John 2:27:

> "And as for you, the anointing which you received from Him abides in you, and YOU HAVE NO NEED FOR ANYONE TO TEACH YOU; but His anointing teaches you about all things, and is true and is not a lie, and just as it has taught you, you abide in Him." (Emphasis is mine)

My purpose here is to encourage people and to build faith for healing. I know what it feels like to be so, so sick, for so, so long, that you feel emotionally fatigued. It helps greatly for someone to remind you of what you know already. Or maybe supply some small missing piece that has eluded you. I have no doubt that you could all do the same for me.

Another point I want to make is that truth exists all at once. It's like the human body; you can't take it apart without it being a problem—smile. You can describe the body, part by part, but it works all at once. Truth is like that. I can describe all the parts of my faith, but it works all at once. As I share the various puzzle pieces of truth that worked for me, I want you to let each piece build in your heart and trust that it will all come together and make a whole picture for you.

Back to the prayer. I want to state once again that I believe it is a legally correct prayer, and that is why it worked for me. The thought arises, "Perhaps it only worked because I believed it would." Since I had prayed numerous prayers prior to this one, which I believed would work but didn't, I don't think it was just about me believing it would work. This prayer has worked for me several times. I believe it is a biblically correct prayer . . . so what could keep it from working? That is what I want to cover next.

1 John 3: 21-22 (New American Standard).

> "Beloved, if our heart does not condemn us, we have confidence before God; And whatever we ask we receive from Him, because we keep His commandments and do the things that are pleasing in His sight."

This is such a simple truth.

If our heart does not condemn us,
we have confidence before God;
and whatever we ask we receive from Him.

If, when you pray, you feel condemnation or unworthiness in your heart, making you feel undeserving, then you will not have confidence before God.

Confidence before God is a great way to say *FAITH*.

As I mentioned in my previous post today, I did a year's worth of EFT regarding the emotions I had that conflicted with what I believed, not only related to healing, but regarding many aspects of my life.

Now I need to clarify this here. I found a verse way back in the beginning of my walk with the Lord that said, "Humble yourself under the mighty hand of God, and He will exalt you at the proper time." I understood that. I knew that Jesus humbled Himself by becoming obedient, even unto the point of death. And I believed that if I did the same and humbled myself by becoming obedient to God, it would pay off at the proper time; so I started on that path and stayed on it, and saw a lot of healing and blessings as a result. It became my lifestyle. Nevertheless, I got sick and couldn't get well. All the spiritual techniques I had used to get well in the past did not work. I was missing it somewhere and didn't know where.

When that goes on for a long time, you can't help but have "feelings" that you are missing it in some way that has displeased God. And, as a result, He just isn't going to heal you. Yet when I prayed and asked for clairty (being willing to correct anything that needed correcting), I never got any direction, because our right to healing is not based on our soulish perfection, but on what Christ purchased for us. Even though I was actually in right standing with God, I didn't FEEL like I was.

Eventually, I realized that God was NOT withholding healing because I wasn't perfect. The problem was what Gary Craig (who coined the phrase Emotional Freedom Technique or EFT) calls "tailenders." It goes something like this:

Out of your head/mouth comes,
    "I'm a lender and not a borrower."

While, at the same time, in your emotions you feel,
"I don't deserve to be free financially."

That is what was happening with me regarding healing. In my belief system, I had: "God wants me well," yet somewhere in the background, in my emotions, I *felt*: "God is displeased with me for some unknown reason." I felt this in spite of the fact that I was walking closely with Him. This is just one of the many lying emotions I had. They were all piled up inside me, making it impossible for me to pray a prayer that I believed, so that I could receive.

This is where EFT came in.

I first awakened to the nearly miraculous benefits of EFT as the result of a desperate prayer. My brother died unexpectedly, and it was devastating to me. For the first time in my relationship with the Lord I felt like I was sinking, possibly never to rise again. I felt such deep grief, saness, nausea and weakness that I was down in bed, feeling like I was sinking into a hole inside me that was so deep it would engulf me.

It was Sunday morning, and I was home alone. I was lying down, and I could feel myself sinking further and further emotionally. I thought about going to the phone and asking a friend to pray for me. However, the thought of saying that my brother had died—well, I felt like if I said it out loud, the grief would be so great that I, literally, would die.

It was a very unusual thing for me. I was accustomed to enjoying emotional buoyancy, even in hard times. But this time none of my normal techniques for encouraging myself were working. Lying there, I told God, "I need help here. I am not dealing well with this, and I seriously need help."

Instantly, I remembered EFT. Though I had only had minor experience with it, I remembered how to do it. I immediately did *one* round saying, "Even though I feel this grief, and sadness and nausea, and profound fatigue, I deeply and completely love and accept myself." By the time I was done tapping on the last acupoints, I felt no grief or sadness, and I had completely normal body energy!

Wow! The whole process took less than two minutes and was a profound experience. I was thrilled, but I was also surprised. First of all, that it worked so well, and second of all, that EFT was the method that God used to help me.

I immediately began to devour all the EFT info I could find. I took the EFT courses offered by Gary Craig, and certified through Patricia Carrington; earning certificates in both basic and advanced EFT. I continued to be thrilled with the remarkable effectiveness of EFT, and daily used it to eliminate every negative emotion that surfaced—no matter how small.

As a result of this remarkable emotional healing, I started to see (as I was seeking God for physical healing) that I had an enormous pile of lying emotions inside me, totally waylaying my faith. I also realized that I could eliminate them with EFT. It was an exciting time. I felt empowered! I had an extremely effective means of eliminating the lying emotions that were conflicting with my faith, and I was extremely eager to use that tool. I began to whittle them away, one by one.

After doing about a year of EFT, I woke up one day and just felt like there were no lying emotions left. I also felt indignant that the enemy had stolen from me for so long, and I felt I could pray, without any *tailenders,* and *believe that I received.* I did pray, and I did believe, and I did receive.

Next week (next chapter) I will share some of the EFT statements that I did during that time. I want you to know, however, that it doesn't have to take a year for you to come to the place of faith and healing. It took me that long, because I was figuring it out as I went. I believe a person could do it much quicker than I did.

EFT is just one way a person can work to see that their heart does not condemn them. Obviously, if you are beating your wife or cheating on your husband; or stealing from your boss; or, or, or, you are probably not going to feel real great about showing up in front of God asking Him to help you out. You might need to do a different kind of work then. However, even if you have obvious reasons to be ashamed, if you realize that no one is perfect enough to earn a healing, and throw yourself on the mercy of the court, in faith, knowing that Christ earned your healing for you, you can be healed in an instant.

For those who *feel* like they don't deserve to be healed, and aren't able to receive because they feel unworthy, EFT can be a great help.

Message Seven

If Your Heart Does Not Condemn You Part 2

*T*oday I will share some of the EFT phrases I worked on. I did not do these non-stop, every day or even every week. I did them as they came up.

I'd also like to say that I had no idea I had so much stuffed emotion. I tended to ignore negative emotions that I knew were non-fruitful. I walked according to what I believed, and ignored emotions that conflicted with what I believed. I assumed that denying/ignoring those emotions meant they left. They didn't; they just went underground, coloring everything I experienced in life, and influencing all my decisions, without me even being conscious that it was happening. The freedom I have experienced, as a result of eliminating all these unhealed emotions, is profound, and I highly recommend EFT to anyone who feels like they are living below their potential in Christ.

As I began to do EFT, I came to see that, when I consciously acknowledged an emotion and eliminated it, another emotion would come to the surface right behind it. Sort of like pulling on a tissue and having another tissue pop up. Sometimes, something that happened in my day would spark something and, instead of ignoring it, I would do EFT for it. As one issue was eliminated, something else would come to mind related to it, and I'd just keep eliminating each issue until I felt clear. Sometimes a session would involve 3 EFT statements; other times it would involve 40. I had a few 2-3 hour sessions, but most were just five minutes or less.

This might sound like an arduous affair, and something you'd like to avoid, but it wasn't for me. I deeply enjoyed the whole process. I was so happy to be feeling lighter and lighter, and freer and freer. It truly was a joyful, liberating, empowering experience. It was "laugh out loud" material for me.

I will now share some of the issues I had, and perhaps they will spark some of your own emotions that you have ignored that are keeping you stuck. I recommend working on what is obvious and know that as you do so, more and more will come up, until one day nothing is coming up. Also, during that time be working on the scriptures that say healing belongs to you—meditating on them and making them a part of your self-image.

Below I will demonstrate one full EFT statement to show the basic form. All the following statements will be the *"issue"* only, and not the full statement. You will see what I mean, as we go.

Example of the full statement with issue underlined:

Even though I feel like <u>*God has let me down*</u>, **I deeply and completely love and accept myself.**

When I am doing a statement like this, I don't try to hide my feelings from God. He knows that I love Him, and I'm expressing a feeling, not a belief. I often say, "I'm sorry God, I know You are good and that You haven't let me down, but I have this *feeling*, and I thank You for helping me eliminate it." The truth is that He knew that feeling was there before I did, and is glad I am getting rid of it.

(For a free download of full instructions on EFT go to: www.fol-hs.com)

Here are some statements you might like to try for yourself:

Even though I:

feel like I don't deserve to be well.

feel like I can't be healed.

feel afraid that God won't heal me.

feel like God doesn't want to heal me.

feel like God is withholding.

am afraid that even God can't fix me.

feel like God doesn't love me in this area.

feel powerless to help myself.

feel like I can't get what I need from God.

feel like I have to be perfect to be healed,
and I can't be perfect, so I can't be healed.

feel hurt because God hasn't healed me.

don't understand what is hampering me.

feel like God is unhappy with me somewhere, or else He
would heal me.

feel like something bad in me is blocking my healing.

feel like I'm missing it somewhere or else God would heal me.

feel like there is some reason God doesn't want to heal me.

feel like I am "un-healable."

Hopefully, this is helping you to get the idea.

Even though I felt like I had a good relationship with the Lord, I also
felt this *unworthiness* thing that I could not put my finger on. I never
got any leading from the Lord that I was missing it anywhere, but I still
felt like I didn't deserve to be healed. In the end, it wasn't God
convicting me of some secret sin; it was just emotional junk that had
nothing to do with reality. Now all those feelings seem foreign to me,
because I whittled them all away, one by one.

The adversary also is the accuser of believers, and sometimes you need to overcome him by the Word of your testimony. In other words, sometimes you just need to say out-loud, "God is good, and I trust Him, and I don't believe the enemy's lies." Then tell him to leave you in the name of Jesus Christ. He is interested in getting you to complain about God, and wants to keep you in a place of doubt and unbelief. If you stand firm and openly state that you trust God, the enemy just isn't interested in hanging around.

The foundational truth is that through Christ my sins are forgiven. And, because of that, I have a right to be well; even if my flesh is not perfect. I am not under the curse, and God is not withholding for some unknown reason.

Some people say, "Well it's just timing. When the time is right, you'll be well." Well, I think that is natural human thinking and is not based on Biblical truth. Jesus never sent anyone away saying, "Well, it's not quite the right time for you," or, "You need to learn compassion, so go suffer for a little while longer," or, "You aren't spiritual enough, so go and grow up and then come back," or "You have hidden sin you need to confess," etc. He always said something along the lines of, "Your faith has healed you."

We have all these natural-thinking ideas about why we aren't getting healed—excuses or explanations—because we just can't figure out why we aren't getting healed. We believe God heals, and we believe He wants to heal us, but we aren't well, so we try to figure it out and some of our explanations sound spiritual, but they really are not.

The truth is that sometimes we are just missing it by not praying correctly. It isn't about hidden sin, or the need to develop compassion, or the need to grow spiritually, blah, blah, blah. It is simply about not praying right, or not believing we have received, because we don't *feel* like we deserve to be healed. This is where EFT can be very helpful.

You can also eliminate those lying emotions through prayer. I have done it many times over the years. I have felt angry with God on occasion—the height of stupidity, I realized—so I would go to God and say, "Lord, I know it is insane to be angry at You. I know You are pure good, and the problem is on my end, but I can't seem to stop, so can You please get this thing off of me?" Usually, the anger would instantly disappear. It has been decades now since I've had that feeling.

Either way, through prayer or prayer with EFT, it helps to get rid of the lying emotions. In fact, EFT statements are always a form of prayer for me. I hit it from the body angle, and the spiritual angle, at the same time. I often tap on the EFT acupoints, while I pray.

Message Eight

If Your Heart Does Not Condemn You Part 3

*R*eady for another piece of the *Truth About Healing* puzzle? Just keep tucking each piece away in your heart and letting it feed your faith, until the pieces come together and make a whole picture that makes sense in your heart.

I want to go back to the verse in 1 John 3:21 that says,

> "Beloved, if our heart does not condemn us, we have confidence before God. And whatever we ask we receive from Him, because we keep His commandments and do the things that are pleasing in His sight."

This is, without a doubt, one of the greatest obstacles to believing and receiving:

SELF-CONDEMNATION

If you don't *feel* like you deserve healing, you will find it difficult to pray with confidence and believe you receive.

I already covered the fact that we can have lying emotions that conflict with what we believe, and that praying and doing EFT can relieve us of those lying emotions. This made an enormous difference for me. My condemnation did not stem from being disobedient, or lazy in my relationship with the Lord. It was totally a false reality, so I was helped greatly by EFT. There may be some readers, however, who have other reasons to feel self-condemnation, so I want to talk about a few other reasons why a person might not have confidence to come before God and ask for help.

If you are not walking with God in the way that you believe He wants you to, your heart will condemn you; and you are probably not going to be able to pray with confidence, until you straighten it out between the two of you. That being said, I've seen some real rascals easily get healed because they had no illusions about their goodness. They truly were repentant and threw themselves on the mercy of the court and were able to trust in God's great compassion. They connected with His forgiveness, and His willingness to do for them what they could not do for themselves, and they were healed.

Non-Christians on the street almost always get healed fast, while Christians struggle to receive. Why? I think it is mainly because people on the street think they are doing fine spiritually, and don't have an overgrown sense of guilt. I also think there is a special healing anointing that accompanies evangelism, which makes it easier. I could be wrong on that, so don't quote me. What I do know is that Christians quite often pray wrong and then decide that the reason they didn't get healed is because God is withholding, due to their imperfection.

We need to know that we can never be perfect enough to *earn* healing. We don't get the blessings of God by being perfect. We receive them as a gift. When Jesus said to the paralytic, "Your sins are forgiven," He was making a statement that healing is yours because your sins are forgiven. He was also making the statement that He had the authority to forgive sins. Most people understand the authority to forgive that He demonstrated, but they don't understand that if their sins are forgiven, they have a legal right to be well.

When I was first ill, I was *seriously* ill—fighting for my life daily—for months on end. One day while I was crying out to Jesus for help, I suddenly felt Him in the room. It seemed as though He was above me to the left, near the ceiling. He clearly spoke to me saying, "Your sins are forgiven." Perturbed, I said, "What does that have to do with anything? I know my sins are forgiven, and I am glad, but I want to be healed." I wanted Him to say, "You are healed." I didn't understand that because my sins were forgiven I had a right to be healed.

He said to me again, "Your sins are forgiven." I was so frustrated and said, "I don't understand." Immediately, He showed me—as clear as clear could be—that, because my sins were forgiven, I was totally free (legally) from all the power of darkness, and there was *no* barrier between God and me. I was spiritually free. Satan had no right to afflict me in any way, and I was completely pure in the eyes of God. I knew that meant I had a legal right to be well. Sadly, I still didn't know how to receive the healing that I had a legal right to. I spent 18 years confused about it. Eventually, I figured out that I needed to enforce my legal position, and command the enemy to go and take his sickness with him; instead of asking God to heal me. When I finally figured that out, I did just that and was healed instantly.

There are only two realities: the Kingdom of Light and the kingdom of darkness, and they are NOT symbolic; they are literal. Kingdom reality is very black and white, which is why Jesus said, "You are either with Me or against Me," and, "you either gather with Me or you scatter." It might be grey in our minds and perceptions, but the truth is that we are either exercising our authority as citizens of the Kingdom of Light, or we are passively allowing the kingdom of darkness to oppress us.

If you have chosen to trust your eternal existence to Christ, and have given Him your heart and accepted Him as your Savior, then He has given you new life in your spirit, and "He has delivered you from the domain of darkness and transferred you to the Kingdom of His dear Son." In that Kingdom you have a legal right to be healed, but it doesn't always happen automatically. Sometimes you have to take your rights by exercising your authority. If you go back and read my prayer, you'll see that I did that. I declared my legal position first, then used my authority to command sickness to go.

If you get it on the inside of you—if you understand your legal position, and you believe in your rights as a forgiven child of God, you will have faith for your healing.

1 John 1:8-9:

> "If we say that we have no sin, we are deceiving ourselves, and the truth is not in us. If we confess our sins, He is faithful and righteous to forgive us our sins and to cleanse us from all unrighteousness."

39

If you have acted on that verse:

> your sins are forgiven,
> you're not under the curse,
> you have been redeemed from sickness,
> you have authority over all the power of the enemy,
> you are in covenant with God,
> all the promises belong to you,
> healing is a promise of God,
> and healing belongs to you.

If you walk in obedience, it will increase your confidence before God. But if you haven't been, and are just now figuring this out, you can go to God and confess your inability to be perfect, and get back on track immediately.

Okay, so you are starting to *get it,* but you still *feel* some condemnation in your heart. Well, let's go back to John 3:21-22. It says, if our heart does not condemn us, we have confidence before God. Let's read some of the earlier verses and see what the context is.

> Verse 18 says, "Little children, let us not love with word or with tongue, but in deed and truth.
> 19 We shall know by this (that we walk in love) that we are of the truth, and SHALL ASSURE OUR HEART BEFORE HIM.
> 20 in whatever our heart condemns us; for God is greater than our heart, and knows all things.
> 21 Beloved, if our heart does not condemn us, we have confidence before God;
> 22 and whatever we ask we receive from Him, because we keep His commandments and do the things that are pleasing in His sight.
> 23 And this is His commandment, that we believe in the name of His son Jesus Christ, and love one another, just as He commanded us."

There are so many points here. For now, however, I want you to see that walking in love gives you confidence before God.

Under both the old covenant and the new covenant, the number one rule/commandment is: love God with all your heart, soul, mind and strength, and your neighbor as yourself. If you can get this one simple fact/truth, you will be on your way to remarkable freedom and fulfillment in all areas of your life, not just regarding your health. You will be lining yourself up for great blessings.

There is no law, man-made or spiritual, which you can break if you walk in love. Walking in love makes you a free person. The number one endeavor for a believer, above all other endeavors, should be to get a revelation of the love commandment and walk it out, whether you are sick or not.

Psalm 72:17 says, *Let men bless themselves by Him.*

When you choose to walk through life according to what God says is true, rather than according to what you perceive to be true, you bless yourself by Him, and there is no greater truth than *Love the Lord your God, and your neighbor as yourself.* That is the highest, purest truth there is. It doesn't get any more profound than this, and anyone with a willing heart can play.

IQ is not an issue
Money is not an issue
Location is not an issue
Status is not an issue
Education is not an issue

Love is the great equalizer. It empowers the lowest of the low to rise to their highest, fullest potential. Love enables the weak to become strong. It sets you free and enables you to help others get free.

God is not on an ego trip!

He instructs you to love Him because He knows that He has got what you want, and loving Him connects you to Him and all that He has— and He has everything good. He lacks no good thing.

If you have given your heart to Christ, then you are born again from above. In the spirit, you are brand new. You have been made a new creation in Christ and are the righteousness of God in Christ. Love is your new nature, and you can draw upon it anytime you choose. If, however, you do not walk in love, you might not have confidence that He has heard you or that you have what you have asked for. The simple solution is to get with Him and get it cleared up. Through repentance and forgiveness, your heart confidence can be restored.

1 Timothy 1:5 says,

> "The goal of our instruction is love from a pure heart and a good conscience and a sincere faith."

Love, from a pure heart and a good conscience and a sincere faith, is our goal.

This is it folks. This is as deep as it gets.

There is a non-Bible proverb that says,

> "The goal is the path."

I think it fits here. Love is the goal of our instruction, but it is also our path.

Is 43:26 says,

> "Put Me in remembrance; let us argue our case together, state your cause that you may be proved right."

If you walk in love, in obedience to the Love Commandment, then you can confidently go to God and argue your case before Him.

Remember that we are not talking legalism and religion here. We are talking about a love relationship.

Walking in love gives you great confidence
in your relationship with God.

He wants to bless you.
And even if you are a nasty little so and so,
if you repent, He is eager to bless you.

Jesus paid for all your sins:
past, present, and future.

You are forgiven.

You are not under the curse.

Sickness is a result of the curse.

You are the righteousness of God in Christ Jesus.

All the promises of God are yes in Christ.

Healing is a promise of God.

Healing is "Yes "in Christ.

Your sins are forgiven.

Sickness has no legal right to stay in your body.

You have a covenant right to health.

Jesus bore your sin—
He became sin for you, so that you could
be the righteousness of God in Him.

Jesus bore your sin and the result of your sin.
He bore your sickness and disease and pain.
By His stripes you were healed. (Peter)

Jesus is the will of God in action.

Jesus said,

"I came down from Heaven, not to do My own will,
but the will of Him who sent Me."

Jesus came down to do God's will.

Jesus healed all who came to Him.

It is God's will for all to be healed.

If your heart does not condemn you,
you can have whatever you ask.

If you haven't been walking in love, don't stay in condemnation. Go to Him and ask for forgiveness. Accept that you are forgiven, and move forward. Begin to believe you receive.

Mark 11:23-24:

> "Truly I say to you, whoever says to this mountain, 'Be taken up and cast into the sea,' and **does not doubt in his heart,** but believes that what he says is going to happen, it shall be granted to him.

> "Therefore I say to you, all things for which you pray and ask, believe that you have received them, and they shall be granted you."

BELIEVE that you **RECEIVE.**

It doesn't say **PERCEIVE** that you **RECEIVE.**

Believing is not about your feelings. It is about knowing who you are in Christ, and knowing what legally belongs to you. It is not about emotions and perceptions. It is about being little children and trusting that Jesus is not a liar and that He truly is the revealed will of God in action. He came to set the captives free. Sickness is a prison, and you have the right to get out of prison. Your sins are forgiven!

Jesus healed ALL who came to Him.

He said, "Your faith has healed you."

Don't fret over the parts that are not yet clear to you. Perhaps you "get it" now. Perhaps you are in the process of "getting it."

Just let it be okay
that you know sickness is not of God,
and that you have hope in your heart.

You can believe and receive your healing now if you are ready. If not, just keep reading, and let your heart soar.

Message Nine

One Way I Was Missing It

Not believing I received, *before* I saw or felt that I was healed, is one way I missed it. Like many others, I would pray, and if I didn't immediately *feel* healed, or *feel* the presence or power of God, I assumed that I had missed it. That led to *feeling* like God didn't answer my prayer, and the presumption that I wasn't praying correctly or didn't deserve to be healed or, or, or. Essentially, I was in doubt, so I would pray again, hoping that I'd get it this time, and on and on it went.

In the process of asking God where I was missing it, I came to understand that this was a fundamental reason for my failure to receive. I was not believing that I *had* received, regardless of how I felt; I was believing that I was *going* to receive, and thinking I would know I was healed by how I felt. Sometimes it goes that way (you feel it and know it), and sometimes you feel nothing and need to believe you receive anyway. When you do, it will often manifest rather quickly, if not instantly.

Once you have prayed a prayer that you know is correct, legally, you can have confidence that He has heard you, and since He has heard you, you have the requests that you have asked of Him. At that point, you need to believe that He has heard and that you do have a yes answer, even if you don't see an instant manifestation. You do this by having confidence in your legal position; not by having some emotional faith feeling. Confidence in your legal position is faith.

I don't know why it sometimes works instantly, and other times it takes days for the healing to manifest, but it does. I suspect that sometimes healing virtue is released into our body and starts the process of healing, but takes a few days to complete the healing.

I remember Kenneth Hagin saying that almost everyone he prayed for with cancer got healed, yet it almost never manifested at the moment he prayed for the person. Generally, it took between 8 to 13 days before it was obvious that it was done.

I do know that believing you have what you have asked for—now—is an enormous part of receiving, and sometimes you have to do that for awhile before you see the answer. Sometimes, boldly and confidently declaring that you are healed, before you see the manifestation, is a part of *believing you have received*. After I figured this out and was healed, I came across a couple of stories that confirmed this for me.

One was about a woman who had been all over the United States asking for prayer for a skin cancer. She had gone to all the big healing meetings she could get to. She had literally been to every minister with a healing gift that she could find. When she was at the last one, he recognized what her problem was and told her he would not pray for her. She was quite shocked. He went on to tell her that if praying for her was going to work, it would have, and that he felt led of the Lord to tell her to go home and say out loud each day, for the next ten days, "According to the Word, I am healed." He explained to her that since she had prayed in accordance with the Word, the Word says she was healed (Is 53 and more). Wisely, she opted to trust him. She said, "Okay," and she went home and did it. All day long, every day, whenever she would think of it she confessed,

"According to the Word, I am healed.

I thank you Lord!

According to the Word, I am healed."

On the thirteenth day, she was in the kitchen sweeping the floor and continuing to declare, "according to the Word I am healed," when the cancer suddenly fell out of her face onto the floor. On her face, where the cancer had been, she had beautiful brand new skin.

I'm sure that on the first day she began to agree with the Word, the healing began, but it took more than a week to complete the healing. Because she stated her legal position, her vital position changed.

Based on this woman's experience, I chose to do the same thing. I prayed and then I declared, "I believe that according to the Word I am healed." It was the only part of the prayer I repeated, and I was prepared to repeat that part until my healing manifested, no matter how long it took. Fortunately, for me, I only had to say it once before I felt the power of God begin to flow. I kept saying it and the power kept getting stronger. And I kept saying it and praising God that, *according to the Word I am healed,* and I kept after it until I knew it was done. I'd say it was less than one minute.

It is not about a magical Christian incantation; it is about believing in your legal position and declaring that your legal position is a reality, even if it hasn't manifested yet. It is very much like this:

> You find out you have an inheritance, and all you have to do to receive your inheritance is to call and claim it, so, you call and request it, and they say, "It is on its way. We have done an electronic funds transfer, and it will be in your account in three to five days." At that point, you can confidently say you have a specific amount of money, even if it isn't in your bank account yet. You have it, and you know, that you know, that you know, that it is real.

Similarly, you have an inheritance in Christ, and part of that inheritance is healing. It is not figurative; it is literal. You have a legal right to claim healing, and to believe that you have received what you have asked for. The moment you believe, the transfer begins— though the full manifestation might not be obvious for a minute or an hour, or a couple of days. You can have the same confidence in this that you would have if someone told you in the natural that they have wired your inheritance money to you.

Unfortunately, for many people, the truth of their healing is no more real to them than the imaginary money in the bank we talked about above, because they don't know that they have a legal right to healing. This *is* their inheritance in Christ, and they *have* a legal right to claim it. If you spend enough time reading what Jesus the Christ purchased for you, and let it sink into your heart that you are not perfect but you are forgiven, and Jesus really did live and breathe and walk this earth and backed up His claims with power; and He really is the same today as He was yesterday; and He really does love you; and He really does want you well; and He really isn't withholding healing, your faith will start to rise. You can pray and believe you receive; not based on emotion, but based on confidence in the historical reality of Christ, and belief in the current legal position you have in Christ.

My next story is about receiving Christ as your Savior, but it also relates to receiving healing. I'm going to quote this one directly from a book called, *How to Turn Your Faith Loose* by Kenneth E. Hagin.

Begin quote:

> Once while I was preaching in Dallas, a man in the church said to me, "We men have an early morning prayer meeting before we go to work each day. One man has been coming five days a week for six months and has been praying, but he is still unsaved. I think you could help him."

> I was introduced to the man during a special Saturday night teaching class, and the moment I looked at him, I knew exactly what was wrong. During the testimony service, I said to him, "Stand and testify, and confess that you're saved."

> He was startled. He looked around, stammering and stuttering a little, then finally said, "Well, I'm not saved yet."

> I said, "You've got your Bible there in your hand, haven't you? Open it to Romans 10:9-10 and read aloud."

> He read, "That if though shalt confess with thy mouth the Lord Jesus, and shalt believe in thine heart that God hath raised him from the dead; thou shalt be saved. For with the heart man believeth unto righteousness; and with the mouth confession is made unto salvation."

> I asked him to repeat the last phrase, "and with the mouth confession is made unto salvation." I said, "Certainly you can't be saved until you confess. It's with the mouth that confession is made. Now stand and confess that you are saved."

"Well," he said, "I don't feel I'm saved."

"Certainly not," I said. "You can't feel something you don't have. And you can't have it until you confess it."

"I don't much believe I want to do that," he answered.

I said, "I understand that you've been coming to this church and praying for six months."

"I sure have," he said. "I've wept and repented for six months."

I said, "All you lack is to stand on this verse. Stand up and confess that."

He *said, "Well, I do believe these verses, that Jesus died for my sins and that He was raised from the dead. God raised Him up for my justification, so I just take Him as my Savior and confess Him as my Lord." Then* he quickly sat down. After a few minutes, he began to glow, and suddenly he began shouting. He later told me, "When I confessed that, something happened inside of me."

I said, "Yes, eternal life was imparted to your spirit."

(He goes on to say,)

So there must be a public confession, for this signals our break with the world. It signals a change of lordship. It defines our position. The confession of the lordship of Jesus immediately puts us under His supervision, care, and protection.

End quotes.

Well, I hope you are getting what I am saying. You believe you receive before you see the manifestation of what you are praying for. The point Kenneth Hagin made about speaking it out is also a point well taken. Openly declaring, "according to Your Word, I am healed," helps us to believe we receive, because the Word of God is filled with the power of God, and our spirit connects with the Holy Spirit when we speak the truth. In addition to that, God has spoken and said, "Say to them, 'As I live,' says the LORD, 'just as you have spoken in My hearing, so I will surely do to you;" That is in Numbers 14:28, the New American Standard version.

I know it doesn't make sense to the natural mind; it is a spiritually appraised truth, but you can do it because you are a spirit being and a being of faith. Faith is your true nature, if you are a Christian. You can simply, with childlike confidence in God's revealed truth, trust that He wants you well and that you have a right to the healing Jesus purchased for you. Then you can tell sickness to go, command your body to be healed, confess that you are healed, believe that He has heard you, believe that you have the thing you have asked for, and you then thank Him for it and you will have it.

What we are not supposed to do is pray, and pray, and pray, and beg, and beg, and beg, and feel like we haven't been heard if it doesn't instantly manifest. We pray (command), then thank Him—repeatedly if need be—to stay in a place of believing for the truth that we "have it," and we will "have it."

It's not about straining; it is about resting in your legal position. When you order something, which is being shipped by mail, you expect it to arrive. In the same way, if you are walking in obedience to the Lord (not perfect, but forgiven), you can stand on your legal rights and you can expect them to become reality in your life. You can expect them to show up, just like a package in the mail.

Use your imagination. This is a very Godly use of the imagination. Imagine that He has heard you, and you have what you have asked for. But don't pray until you really know that the Word says healing belongs to you. When you have confidence in your legal position, THEN pray.

Confidence in your legal position is faith. Faith is not some nebulous emotional feeling that God will heal you. Faith is simple childlike confidence in God's character and your legal position. That confidence *can* evoke positive emotions, but the emotion is not what gets it for you. It is your choice to believe that allows you to receive any promise in the Word.

Your sins are forgiven,

You are not under the curse,

Jesus became a curse for you,

Sickness is part of the curse,

Sickness has no legal right to stay in your body,

You are the righteousness of God in Christ Jesus,

All the promises of God are yes in Christ,

Healing is a promise of God,

Healing is yes in Jesus.

Meditate on these truths from the Word, and you will begin to trust that they apply to you. Just the fact that you hope they do should tell you that it is right. You know in your heart that sickness is miserable and tormenting and not from a loving God.

God is love.

He is compassionate.

His mercies never fail.

He is our healer.

He is not withholding.

One Way I Was Missing It

Message Ten

Single-Minded

I had some trouble with what to put in the subject line of this post.

Change Your Mind—Renew Your Mind—Be Transformed?

I want to talk about the issue of *heart condemnation* from a somewhat different angle. 2 Corinthians 5:16 instruct us to "know no man after the flesh." We are to see others as New Creations in Christ, rather than thinking their flesh is who they really are. I believe it is just as necessary for us to not know ourselves after the flesh. Instead, it is imperative that we see ourselves as New Creations in Christ.

What is the flesh, anyway? It is your body under the influence of the adversary. It is your body affected by diet, life experiences, hormones and more. YOU are a spirit who lives in a body, and your flesh is your senses under the influence of the enemy—the god of this world, the ruler of the kingdom of darkness. It is also your sub-conscious. It is your lifetime collection of memories that have trained you to experience automated biological feelings/responses to everything in life. If you mistakenly think that your biological desires and responses (programmed into your cells as you experience life) are who you really are, then you will have a good bit of self-condemnation.

There is another verse that says, "The mind set on the flesh is death." Why? Our bodies often desire things, which are not good for us, or it. Addictions to drugs, food, pornography, TV, computer games and novels, etc., are all flesh issues, of course. The flesh can also be seen in things like fear and depression, and confusion. If you see those as the real *you* (and own them), then you are sunk in the water.

James 1:22 and following:

> "But prove yourselves doers of the Word and not merely hearers who delude themselves. For if anyone is a hearer of the Word and not a doer, he is like a man who looks at his natural face in a mirror, for once he has looked at himself and gone away he has immediately forgotten what kind of a person he was."

The reason some people don't do the Word is because they believe that their flesh is who they really are; instead of seeing themselves as righteous New Creations in Christ. If you really believe that you are a New Creation, you will want to live from that reality. On the other hand, if you believe that your flesh is the real you, then you will feel like you have disappointed God, and you'll feel bad about yourself; you will feel heart condemnation.

You are not your flesh!
You are a New Creation in Christ.
You are a spirit that will live forever, long after your body dies.
Your spirit has been restored and
you are "the righteousness of God in Christ Jesus."
The Spirit of life in Jesus Christ
has set you free from the law of sin and death.
You have been transferred to the Kingdom of Light.
You have the mind of Christ.

Okay, stick with me here. We just read James 1:22-24. Let's go back a few verses to James 1:5-8:

> "But if any of you lacks wisdom, let him ask of God, Who gives to all men generously and without reproach, and it will be given to him.
>
> But let him ask in faith without any doubting, for the one who doubts is like the surf of the sea, driven and tossed by the wind.
>
> For let not that man expect that he will receive anything from the Lord, being a double-minded man unstable in all his ways."

I'm going to rephrase this.

If you want to receive anything from God, you need to be single-minded and ask in faith. When you do, God, Who gives to all men generously, will give you what you ask for. If you are not single-minded, you will not receive from God. In addition, you will be unstable in all your ways.

Single-mindedness and faith go together.

Double-mindedness occurs
when we vacillate between
the mind of Christ and the mind of the flesh.

Single-mindedness occurs
when you look at yourself in the mirror of the Word,
and believe what it says about you,
and recognize that *YOU* are not your flesh.

You are an eternal, recreated spirit
and your flesh is your challenge, it is not the real you.

(NOTE: Yielding to our flesh can send us to hell, so we cannot stand in front of God and say, "It wasn't me, it was my flesh." We are instructed to walk after the Spirit and not after the flesh, for this very reason. Because we are spirits, we are not supposed to be body dominated.)

Romans 12:2 says:

"Do not be conformed to this world, but be transformed by the renewing of your mind."

You transform your flesh by renewing the mind of the flesh. You look in the mirror of the Word, see who you are, believe it is true and, by faith, walk according to that. When you do that, your flesh falls in line with your spirit, and you are transformed.

James goes on to say in 4:8:

" . . . purify your hearts, you double-minded."

When you choose to walk according to what the Word says about you, it will purify the heart of your flesh and will make you more and more single-minded. If you mistakenly think that your flesh is who you really are, then you will feel condemnation, AND you will be double-minded, and receiving from God becomes far more difficult.

In studying natural medicine through the Global College of Natural Medicine, I was required to listen to a CD series by Dr. Weil where he taught about the body-mind connection—how the mind affects the body. He shared about two people diagnosed with multiple personality disorders. One patient was a severe insulin-dependent diabetic (who had to do injections of insulin daily) in one personality but had no blood sugar problems at all when manifesting his secondary personality. Think about that; one body, but two totally different states of health, depending on which mind was in control. Wow!

I'll play some Jeopardy music here while you ponder that one.

♪ ♫ ♪

There was another man who had a serious citrus allergy in one personality, and in the other, he could eat oranges all day long with no ill effects. Think about that. Just by switching from one mind to another, these two people were either very sick or not sick at all.

Now consider that Christians also have two personalities or minds. They have the mind of the flesh and the mind of Christ. In your body, you have a brain that has been trained since birth to think and act according to natural training, but you are also filled with the Holy Spirit and have the mind of Christ. You can access either mind, and you can also vacillate between the two minds.

If you think that having the mind of Christ is figurative, and your flesh is who you really are, you are not going to have faith; you will experience self-condemnation. However, if you choose to live a spirit-dominated life, your confidence will be in what the Word says, rather than what you feel, and you will enjoy faith. You can live from the mind of Christ and live in excellent health.

You might have seen my next example in the news. It was about a woman who was a recipient of a heart transplant. She was pretty much a salad-eating kind of girl. However, after she had a heart transplant, she craved Colonel Sanders' Chicken, and the first thing she did when she got out of the hospital was to go and get a bucketful and chow down.

Also, after her transplant, she became obsessed with a particular sport and a particular team from a different State than the one she lived in. Later, it was revealed that her heart donor was a young man who went to that particular school, and loved that sport, and was 'addicted' to Colonel Sanders' chicken. So now, she not only has her own flesh to deal with, but now she has his flesh influencing her also. Pause and think about that one.

How is this possible? Because, memory and emotional desires are stored in cells, and she received an enormous amount of neurons when she received his heart—neurons filled with memories and stored emotions, which included his physical cravings. Her experience is not uncommon. It happens with all heart transplant patients, from what I have read. Some even have clear memories from their donor; remembering poems or names, etc.

As I said before, life experiences, diet, toxicity, hormones, light, and more affect our flesh. If we could go back in time and grow up in a foreign country, we would be quite different than we are now. We would like different foods and colors, and music, etc.

> You are an eternal spirit,
> and if YOU belong to Christ
> YOU are profoundly different than YOU were
> before YOU received Christ,
> and YOU are not your body.

I would encourage you to get some notebook paper, open up the New Testament and begin to write down everything it says you are or have, in Christ. For those who are not inclined to put out that much effort, you might want to get, *Enjoy Your Rights & Privileges Now.* It is a compilation of our rights and privileges in Christ and is available on Amazon, and also on my website:

http://www.donnacrow.com

You will find it under "Books." Another excellent option is a little booklet by Kenneth E Hagin called, *In Him.*

As long as you think that you are merely your body and your natural personality, you will have a low level of faith.

Your flesh can affect you, and you can affect your flesh, and you can choose who has the upper hand. You can look in a natural mirror and think that what you see is the real you. Or you can look into the mirror of the Word and realize that you really do have the mind of Christ, and begin to confess it and utilize it. This builds faith. Seeing your flesh as the real you, will drain the life out of your faith.

"Do not be conformed to this world
but be transformed by the renewing of your mind."

The mind of Christ or the mind of the flesh, it is a choice. Operating from the mind of the flesh, we can be sick, as sick can be. Operating from the mind of Christ, we can be free of all sickness.

Jesus said,

"I have given you authority over all the power of the enemy
and nothing shall in any way harm you."

Jesus spoke to me recently in the middle of the night and said,

"The Word of God powerfully resides within you.
Nothing can harm you unless you refuse to let the Word work."

I asked Him,
"How do I refuse to let the Word work?"

He said,

"By fear. Fear is the opposite of authority.
Simply make a choice: fear or authority."

I said, "I don't understand."

He said,

"You're afraid to speak, because you're afraid it won't work."

End quote.

Do you get that? You take authority with your mouth, and you confess what the Word says about you. You have the right (purchased by Jesus) to take authority over the enemy and the elements. Few of us do, however, because we are afraid it won't work and then we will be embarrassed. When we don't realize who we are in Christ, we will mistakenly think we are our flesh.

Here are a few examples of taking authority:

A friend of mine had a dog that was very dear to her. We were out for a walk, and the dog ran right in front of a truck that was speeding down the road. We were in a very rural setting, and the dog was not on a leash. The truck sort of came out of nowhere and before we could intervene; it was suddenly upon her and hit her, throwing her to the side of the road. Remarkably, she landed on her feet, but she was obviously hurt. We carried her home and put her on her bed and began to exercise authority over any damage. She was a large dog and by the time we got her home, she had a swelling on the side of her body about the size of half a watermelon. It was at least six inches tall and ran the whole length of her side.

Among the many things that I spoke over her, I commanded the swelling to go in the name of Jesus. Instantly, it deflated under my hands. I mean, this gigantic swelling the size of half a large watermelon, sliced from end to end, went flat in one second, faster than a balloon deflating. If I hadn't dared to believe that this was my right, and hadn't *just tried it,* that would not have happened. Because I dared to act on what I believed (instead of what I was feeling), the dog lived and did well.

My friend was also right beside me, praying as fervently and authoritatively as I was. We didn't talk about it; we just jumped in and did what we knew we had a right to do. It pays to know the Word and what belongs to you when life challenges arise.

Another Recent Story . . .

A few months ago I woke up to a major snowstorm. The sky was loaded with dark, dense clouds, and snow began to fall in huge flakes like a thick curtain. I was not happy. I needed to do business and needed to get to the post office that day. I also knew that a late spring snow would be damaging to our local crops like fruit and nut trees. I chose to stir myself up and pray, "God, this can't be happening right now." I commanded the clouds to break up, the snow to stop, and the whole thing to dissipate in the name of Jesus Christ, and that is exactly what happened. It was predicted to go on for a couple of days, but it didn't. The dense mass of dark clouds quickly disappeared, and the snow stopped almost instantly, and I cheerfully went about my business.

When Jesus was asleep in the boat on the lake with the disciples, a severe storm came up, and they began to take on water. The disciples panicked and woke Jesus up and saying, "Master, don't you care that we perish?" He didn't comfort them; He scolded them, asking them why they didn't have faith. He spoke to the storm and said "Peace," and it was instantly calm. He had already been teaching them that nothing could harm them and they could tell a mountain to move and it would literally move, but they thought they were their flesh, and they didn't think they had authority over the weather, so they lived from their flesh and expected *Him* to fix it. He expected *them* to fix it.

You have to get past thinking that your body and its emotions and cravings and fears, are the real you. EFT is very helpful with that. When you do EFT, and negative emotions disappear, it begins to sink in a little bit that what you feel emotionally isn't necessarily the "real" you.

It is time to look in the mirror of the Word and, like the Queen in Alice in Wonderland, start to practice believing the seeming impossibleness of who you really are in Christ. The things impossible with men are possible with God, and all things are possible to him who believes.

Begin to believe that you are forgiven.

You are the righteousness of God in Christ.

You have the mind of Christ.

If you don't have a Bible, you can read it online for free. There are many places where you can do so. Two of my favorites are:

http://www.biblegateway.com and http://www.biblehub.com

I'd recommend starting with the New Testament. As you read and learn what belongs to you, ask yourself if you are enjoying all Kingdom rights that belong to you. Set your heart and mind on what you possess in Christ and begin to walk in your authority, instead of self-condemnation and fear.

Become single-minded about God's will regarding health and healing. Remember that Jesus is God's revealed will and He healed all who came to Him. Do some EFT for that *other* mind that says you can't have it or don't deserve it. Pray and ask God to help you to think in line with His Word. Use your will to choose to believe the truth about your right to be well. You know it is true anyway—in your heart of hearts.

Jesus is God's will revealed
and He heals all who come to Him.

Single-Minded

Message Eleven

Authority Over Power

I want to talk a little about *Authority* vs. *Power.* I mentioned previously that Jesus has given us authority over all the power of the enemy. I want to make the point that God is the one with the power, and we are the ones with the authority. It is an important distinction, in my mind. I haven't heard any teaching on this, but I'm sure it is out there. If it isn't, it should be.

As I said before, we can get all confused in our heads about what we think is real, based on our experience or observations, or just musings, which are not based on the Word (what Jesus or His followers taught). Not being clear about the difference between power and authority can cause confusion and lack of victory. If, when you are trying to receive healing, you are focused on power, rather than authority, it can waylay you.

Here are a couple of scriptures to help clarify:
Luke 10:19, Jesus speaking . . .

> "Behold, I have given you authority to tread upon serpents and scorpions, and over all the power of the enemy, and nothing shall injure you."

Some believers might think this does not apply to us today since He was speaking to the seventy disciples He sent out at that time. I would refer them to Mark 16: 17-18. Jesus said,

> "And these signs will accompany those who have believed; in my Name they will cast out demons, they will speak with new tongues, they will pick up serpents, and if they drink any

deadly poison, it shall not hurt them; they will lay hands on the sick, and they will recover."

He made similar statements in other places, at other times; sometimes including "raise the dead" in the list. I'm wondering how many of you believe that you have the power to raise the dead. Well, you might think you do, but you don't. What? But Jesus said . . .

Well, He said we had **authority,** He did not say power. Just trying to see if you are paying attention. (Smile) There is a difference, and not consciously distinguishing between the two can cause confusion. I mean, if you think you are supposed to have some amazing power to do amazing things, and you know you couldn't make one hair white or black, as Jesus once said, then you will just be confused. If, however, you understand that you have authority that releases God's power, and authority that controls the enemy's power, then you will have clarity and confidence.

I believe we have authority, not power.

God's power dwells in you and is around you, but it is God's power. You are not sorcerers or conjurers. You are children of God, citizens of the Kingdom of light, with legal authority, which, when you exercise it, God backs up with power.

Here is a line from Acts 19:11

"And God was performing extraordinary miracles (literally, "works of power") by the hands of Paul,"

It doesn't say *Paul* was performing extraordinary works of power; it says *God* was.

The following segment is a bit long, but I encourage you to read it all.

John 15, Jesus speaking:

"I am the true vine, and My Father is the vinedresser. Every branch in Me that does not bear fruit, He takes away: and every branch that bears fruit, He prunes it, that it may bear more fruit. You are already clean because of the word, which I have spoken to you. Abide in Me, and I in you. As the branch cannot bear fruit of itself, unless it abides in the vine, so neither can you, unless you abide in Me. I am the vine; you are the branches; he who abides in Me, and I in him, he bears much fruit; for

apart from Me you can do nothing.

If anyone does not abide in Me, he is thrown away as a branch, and dries up; and they gather them, and cast them into the fire, and they are burned. If you abide in Me, and My words abide in you, ask whatever you wish, and it shall be done for you. By this is My Father glorified, that you bear much fruit, and so prove to be My disciples. Just as the Father has loved Me, I have also loved you, abide in My love. If you keep My commandments, you will abide in My love, just as I have kept My Father's commandments, and abide in His love. These things I have spoken to you, that My joy may be in you, and that your joy may be made full."

I think the picture He paints is pretty clear, but, just in case it isn't, I will rephrase it. Jesus is the living plant. He is the roots and the plant itself. We are merely the branches. He is the source of life and power; we are the branches, and His power flows from Him to us, and through us. But, if we are not connected to Him, we are powerless. Apart from Jesus, you can do nothing. The good news is that we are not disconnected from Him, and He gave us authority, and that authority releases His power.

So, imagine that you are going to pray for yourself or for someone else to be healed. If you believe that you are supposed to have power to heal people, then you are going to expect to have some consciousness of that power or some sensation or feeling of it. What happens when you don't? Many people just won't pray. Others might pray, but on the inside they feel like nothing is going to happen; they are just going through the motions. I've been there and done that.

Or, they pray, but if they don't feel anything, they think they didn't get it and they cease to believe they received, and so they don't. For this reason, it is important to know that you have authority, not power.

Authority is power of attorney in Jesus' Name. It isn't an emotional issue. It can involve emotions, but it isn't about feeling something.

You can feel completely flat and still believe that you have authority in Jesus' Name—over all the power of the enemy. You can stand on that authority without any sensation of power or any feeling of the Presence of God.

Remember I told the story of praying for my friend's dog after a car hit it? Well, I will tell you what I felt at that time. I felt compassion for my friend who loved her dog and was totally freaked out. I felt fear that the dog would not live. I felt the panic of an emergency situation. I felt no consciousness of God at all. I mostly felt freaked out, but I knew my rights as a believer, and when I ignored what I was feeling and commanded the swelling to go, in the name of Jesus, it did. And, I was shocked that it worked.

We spoke many other things over the dog, exercising authority over internal bleeding and organ damage, etc. I can't prove it, but there is no reason for me to believe that the other issues responded any differently than the swelling did. Her dog was sore for a few days, but she fully recovered.

The point is, I didn't *feel* any power. I didn't *feel* any Presence of God. I felt all the things you would not want to feel if you thought *you* were your source. Fortunately, Jesus is and was my source, and He was not freaked out, and

HIS power was released
when I exercised *MY* authority,

in spite of how I felt.

Some people do feel the Presence of God when they pray for themselves or others; others do not. Either way, it doesn't matter. What matters is *believing you receive,* based on your covenant rights, and based on the authority Christ has given you. Jesus didn't say, "Whatever you pray *perceiving* you shall receive." He said, whatever you pray *believing* you shall receive."

It is not about power; it is about authority.

As a believer, not a perceiver, you have authority. The power of God is released in response to your Words, when you exercise your authority.

Authority is not a feeling,
it is a legal position.

Well, that is my main point. Get it on the inside of you that you have authority, and that, that authority doesn't necessarily come with any feelings, and decide to begin to exercise your authority. Ask the Holy Spirit to teach you and He will. Jesus said the Holy Spirit would guide us into all truth. Believe that and make use of it.

These things are spiritually understood; they make little sense to the natural mind and require revelation. Perhaps pray the following prayer over yourself on a regular basis and believe you have received the answer to it. This would be a good place to start *believing you receive.*

Ephesians 1: 17-18

Paul prays,

". . . that the God of our Lord Jesus Christ, the Father of glory, may give to you a spirit of wisdom and of revelation in the (true) knowledge of Him.

I pray that the eyes of your heart may be enlightened, so that you may know what is the hope of His calling, what are the riches of the glory of His inheritance in the saints."

Ask the Lord for a spirit of wisdom and revelation in the area of healing and authority. Revelation comes from God. Ask in faith, without doubting, and you will receive wisdom and revelation.

When you get to the point where you are ready to pray for healing, remember that you have authority, which doesn't necessarily come with any feelings or result in any feelings. It does, however, release the power of God.

Stay connected to the Vine, by walking in love. Stick close to Jesus, Who has the power, and He will release it when you exercise your authority.

There is, therefore, now, no condemnation

for those who are in Christ Jesus.

You are in Christ Jesus.

Your sins are forgiven.

You are the righteousness of God in Christ.

You are a child of God.

You are a citizen of the Kingdom of God.

You have covenant rights.

You are not under the curse.

You are in covenant with God.

Healing is one of the benefits
of being in covenant with God.

Sickness has no legal right
to stay in your body.

Jesus told believers to "lay hands on the sick, and they shall recover,"
period. He did not say, lay hands on the sick and:

"If it's God's will they shall recover," or
"If they are prayed up they shall recover," or
"If it is the right time they shall recover," or
'"If their heart is pure enough they shall recover," or
"If they feel the power of God surge through them,
they shall recover."

Jesus is God's will in action.

Jesus healed all who came to Him.

Jesus is the same
yesterday today and forever.

Jesus still heals all who come to Him.

The Father is not withholding.

God has the power; you have the authority.

Authority Over Power

Message Twelve

Tapping Into Truth

I mentioned before that EFT was extremely helpful to me in eliminating emotions that conflicted with what the Word says is true. I want to mention that I also have found it to be amazing to tap on the basic EFT acupressure points while speaking scripture. Generally, I did not quote scripture word for word, but the basic truth of each scripture. If you prefer, however, you could choose specific verses and quote them exactly.

When I tapped while declaring Bible truth, I found that the truth of what I was saying penetrated my heart more than it did when just saying the statements without tapping on the acupressure points. I found it greatly helped me believe what I was saying.

Instead of doing the normal EFT statement of *Even though I_____*, I would just sort of pray scripture over myself and start tapping on the points like you normally would, **tapping on one point for each phrase**, so that you quickly move through the points.

It would go something like this:

I thank You Father that:

> I walk in love and abide in Christ;
> I am loved by my Heavenly Father, Who is good, and Whose mercies never fail;
> I walk in love and I am free;
> I am free from the curse;
> I am the righteousness of God in Christ Jesus;
> Jesus has set me free from the law of sin and death;

I am forgiven;
I am loved;
I don't stress;
I don't strain;
I don't worry;
I let love work;
I flow in the spirit;
Love flows through me;
I am forgiven;
My sins are forgiven;
God has nothing against me;
God is for me;
God is not withholding;
God is trying to help me;
I am in Christ;
Christ is in me;
I am in the light as He is in the light;
I rule and reign in life;
The life of God in me enlightens me;
The Spirit of Christ in me teaches me;
I teach others;
I am free;
I am free from condemnation;
I am in right standing with God;
All the promises of God are yes in Jesus and belong to me;
I have faith, and it pleases God;
I have, and more is given to me;
I am richly blessed;
I teach others and they are blessed;
I preach the good news;
I am free in Christ;
I have liberty in Christ;
I have life more abundantly;
I walk after the spirit,
I do not walk after the flesh;
I rejoice in truth;
I walk in the light of God's truth;
I bless myself by obeying the voice of God;
God is on my side;
God delights to give me the desires of my heart;
I am a believer;
Believing is easy for me;

I have the mind of Christ;
I have a Spirit of wisdom and revelation living inside me;
The anointing of Christ is mine;
I am loved;
I dwell in the light as He is in the light;
I am free;
I am filled with faith.

You get the idea. I don't want to rewrite the entire Bible here. Smile.

You can just start at the top of the list, or make your own list and start tapping on acupressure points while saying these out loud. The trick is to read them with the right brain, instead of the left. In other words, let your heart get involved. Be thanking God that all these statements are true regarding you, and tap while doing it. When you do, it becomes alive in your own heart, and anything that is alive in your own heart releases faith and causes truth to manifest in your life.

Anything that scratches inside, that doesn't feel right, that you feel like you don't believe . . . take that and turn it into an EFT phrase such as, "Even though I don't 'feel' like I am loved, I deeply and completely love and accept myself." Or maybe that needs to be altered to "Even though I don't feel like God loves me, I want to deeply and completely love and accept myself."

Once again, with EFT it is not about what you believe; it is about what you feel. It is not about adult logic; it is about child emotions. You can know that God loves you, but feel like He doesn't. And, if that is true, you won't offend Him by admitting it. He already knows how you feel and wants you free of the lie.

Back to the list.

The first time I did this, the truth of what I was saying (the truth of the teachings of Christ), so penetrated my heart that I found myself weeping a glad weeping, from really knowing that those things were true. There is something about tapping while quoting the scriptures out loud; that causes them to come alive to you. The truth they contain feels real to you. It is like the scripture is attached to an arrow that shoots past your flesh and makes a direct hit in your heart, without any *yah butts* slowing it down.

I really enjoy tapping on truth in this way. Also, it is not about simply speaking the truth. It is about thanking God for the fact that it is your truth. Thanking Him that you are a child of the light and that you are forgiven, etc. It is a prayer of thanksgiving, with tapping added, and it seems to supercharge your faith. Try it and see what you think.

Message Thirteen

Resentment—Gratitude—Praise

In my own life, I discovered that resentment blocks gratitude and, once again, EFT helped me here. When I did EFT for resentment it was like a blockage was removed and suddenly I felt grateful.

Early in my walk with the Lord He told me "grateful hearts receive more." I understood that to mean that gratitude is like a magnet, drawing good things to you. Nevertheless, I still found myself failing to feel as grateful as I should have. I had so much to be grateful for, yet I also had a good deal of lack, and the lack had created resentment which I wasn't even aware of until I began to do EFT for other things. I began to be aware of emotions that I had previously been completely unaware of— such as resentment.

EFT can't take the place of the Word, or Jesus, or the leading of the Holy Spirit, or obedience, etc. It is just a handy tool to use to deal with the flesh, much like balancing hormones to effect the emotions, or eating right to effect emotions, or exercising to effect emotions. None of these are a substitute for God. I have found, however, that my body greatly affects my faith so anything that helps in that area is welcome to me. EFT was handy because I could go to God with statements like:

"Even though I resent the fact that I can't eat whatever I want to,"
"I resent the fact that my diet is so limited,"
"I resent the fact that I have to do ____"
"I can't do _____ " or, or, or.

When I did that, I found my gratitude rising. I started to *feel* the gratitude that was resident in my heart but hidden under piles of resentment. I began to feel genuinely grateful for all the many and varied ways the Lord had blessed me and that is a good thing. Not just because God likes it when you are thankful (though He does), but because gratitude makes God more real to you and that increases your faith. I highly recommend cultivating gratitude and getting rid of resentments through the use of prayer and EFT.

Philippians 4:8 says:

> "Finally brethren, whatever is true, whatever is honorable, whatever is right, whatever is pure, whatever is lovely, whatever is of good repute, if there is any excellence and if anything worthy of praise, let your mind dwell on these things."

I have found that praising God is a real faith builder. When I first start to praise God, I often feel flat. Nevertheless, I start (generally, with some scripture like, "For the Lord, He is good, and His mercies endure forever), and I find that my internal atmosphere alters, and I no longer feel stupid or flat. I quickly move over into enjoying His atmosphere. I've noticed there is something quite powerful about declaring that particular scripture out loud.

Are you familiar with how tuning forks work? If you have two in a room and you strike one, the one you struck will begin to hum, and the tuning fork that you didn't strike will also begin to hum. It is a frequency thing. Sound is frequency, and the frequency from one tuning fork hits the other tuning fork and causes it to vibrate.

When I say the sentence, "For the Lord, He is good, and His mercies endure forever," I can feel it on the inside. It feels like a frequency that is tuning me up. I don't understand it, but it is true for me. I start there and then I just thank Jesus, or the Father, for whatever I can think of that I am thankful for, big or small.

I mean . . . I thank Him for His goodness and kindness and compassion; and that He never leaves us or forsakes us; that His covenant to be our God is established forever, and on, and on, and on. I often sing, which is something only God wants to hear. Chuckle. As I do this, I really start to feel what I'm saying, and I can feel His pleasure and He becomes more real to me, and this is helpful in building faith. I generally do this for 10 minutes to half an hour.

Gratitude works a number of ways. It attracts blessings, it pleases God, it reduces condemnation in my heart, and it makes God more real to me, which increases my faith, and it is not merely a mental exercise. You can be assured that if you spend time praising and thanking God that He will hear, and He will respond. And you can tell when He is satisfied with your praise. He is real and He does connect with us. He does enjoy our praise, and He does reach a point where He is satisfied with our gratefulness, and you can feel it, and when you do, you know you are done.

I want to say again that this does not come naturally to me. I don't think it comes naturally to many people. It is something that requires you to get past your natural feelings and choose to be grateful. When you do, you tap into that place where you truly feel grateful, and God hears and it pleases Him, and it opens the door for more blessings and builds your faith.

Some people might feel more comfortable with getting a praise tape and using it to praise God. I think this is good in its own right, but there is something about non-electric, personal praise out of your heart and mind (no matter how clumsy or awkward it might feel in the beginning) that is powerful and worth pursuing. Conversely, watching secular TV can suck the life out of your faith. There are activities that feed your faith and activities that drain your faith. If you are serious about getting well, you will want to seriously make choices that increase your faith.

It is not about trying to look good enough to God in order to persuade Him to touch you with His magic wand of healing. It is about helping yourself to get past any obstacles you have that keep you from reaching out and taking what He is trying to hand you. If you can be filthy-dirty, cranky, unscrupulous and generally running over with sin, and still manage to have faith in His goodness, then you will receive.

In truth, sometimes people who are not very spiritual receive easier than those who think they have to impress God to be healed. They know they can't impress God and are sometimes better able to tap into His grace and mercy. Nevertheless, praising God is wonderful and can help you to connect with Him.

We can also learn from others who have spent time praising God. David, who wrote many worship songs, is one:

Psalm 103:

> Bless the Lord, O my soul
> And all that is within me,
> bless His holy name.
> Bless the Lord, O my soul,
> And forget none of His benefits;
> Who pardons all my iniquities;
> Who heals all my diseases;
> Who redeems my life from the pit;
> Who crowns me with lovingkindness
> and compassion;
> Who satisfies my years with good things,
> So that my youth is renewed like the eagle.

Notice I changed it to make it personal to me: *My* iniquities and *my* diseases. Also notice that the forgiveness theme is there again, "He forgives all my sins and heals all my diseases." Forgiveness of sins and healing go hand in hand.

Praising God for what He does, and Who He is, can increase your faith and draw His blessings to you.

Doing EFT, under the leading of the Holy Spirit, to eliminate resentments, will increase your connection to the true gratitude in your heart and will draw you closer to the Father. Intentionally spending time in gratitude, praise and thanksgiving can help you move in the direction of the healing you desire.

God's compassionate goodness is truth, and sickness is subject to that truth. Being grateful and praising God helps connect you to His compassionate goodness, and the healing that is legally yours.

Eliminate resentment.

Cultivate gratitude.

Cultivate a habit of Praise and Thanksgiving.

It will make God more real to you
and increase your faith.

Without faith it is impossible to please God.

Faith pleases God

Faith is the substance of things hoped for,
the conviction of things not seen.

You are a BELIEVER.

Believing is your true nature.

All things are possible to the one who believes.

Your faith makes you well.

Gratitude increases your faith.

See: Enjoy Heaven Now, the 3rd volume in The Enjoy Life Now series, for more in-depth teaching on connecting with Heaven through private worship. Available on Amazon and at: http://www.donnacrow.com Available as an E-book on Kindle and also in paperback.

.

Resentment—Gratitude—Praise

Message Fourteen

Surrender

I want to share a little bit about how to increase your understanding of truth. Foundational, of course, is just reading the Word and seeing what Jesus did, and what He taught, and what His disciples did and taught. Often, however, even when we do this, we miss a great deal of the truth that is presented.

Truth does not dawn on anyone's heart all at once. There is a scripture in Proverbs that says, "The path of the righteous is like the light of the dawn shining brighter and brighter until the full day." Truth is like that. It slowly dawns on our heart as we walk in love, pursuing a true knowledge of Jesus and His Kingdom. Nevertheless, there are ways we can increase our understanding, and one major factor is being willing to do God's will.

John 7:17:

> If any man is willing to do His will, he shall know of the teaching, whether it is of God, or whether I speak from Myself.

If you are not willing to do God's will, then the teachings of Christ will not make sense to you, and you won't accept them as being of God. Being willing to do God's will opens your heart to revelation knowledge of the truth being taught. You cannot understand *"love your enemy"* with the natural mind. It is spiritually understood, and that understanding comes when we are willing to do His will..

Lack of surrender leads to lack of understanding. We fail to surrender because we fear what it will cost us. The truth is that not surrendering costs us our freedom and liberty. Christ came to give us life more abundantly, and we can only get it by being surrendered to God. The enemy would have you believe that if you really give your life to Christ, the Father will send you to some country you don't want to go to or will require things of you that will make you miserable, but He doesn't.

You know, God did a rather spectacular job of moving the Israelites out of Egypt. I mean, He did amazing miracles in the process of getting them out of Egypt, then He did amazing miracles of provision while they lived in the wilderness; then He did amazing miracles to get them out of the wilderness into the land of promise; and it was all for what? It was for them to enjoy everyday life, which included:
    some land to live on and raise animals,
    some fruit trees,
    a nice house full of nice things,
    freedom from their enemies,
    health,
    plenty of money,
    fertility,
    peace of mind,
    and productivity.

God did fantastic miracles so they could live a simple, peaceful life, free from slavery. This is His will: a long satisfied life. And He wanted the whole world to observe their blessed lives and awaken to His love and His desire to be God to them and restore what the enemy has stolen.

God has amazing truth in the Word for you, and He has miracles of protection for you; He has miracles of provision for you, and He has miracles of deliverance for you. Not so that He can turn you into someone you don't want to be (whatever your personal fear is), but so that you can live a quite peaceful life, filled with provision, so you can live satisfied and at peace.

The fear is:
    If you truly surrender your whole life to the Lord, He will promptly begin to require things of you that will make you miserable.

The truth is:

If you truly surrender your whole life to the Lord, He will honor His Word and will set about to free you from all the effects of the curse in your life.

God is about families and love and satisfying the desires of your heart. He's about land and fruit trees and peace. He is about children being safe, and marriages being good. He's about setting you free, so you can help others get free. He's about blessing you financially, so you overflow, and can help others who have needs. He's about life more abundantly.

"The eyes of the Lord range to and fro throughout the earth that He may show Himself strong on behalf of the one whose heart is completely His."

Surrender gets God on your side and opens the way for Him to guide you into profound blessing. He will not immediately set about to make you miserable, in an effort to make you spiritual. He will set about to deliver you from darkness. He will set about to show Himself strong on your behalf.

Jesus came to give us life more abundantly, not to make us live lives that feel miserable and foreign to us. If God calls you to go to some distant land to help those in need, it will satisfy your heart beyond your wildest dreams. And He won't call you to it if He hasn't already put it into your heart. He doesn't call us to do stuff that burdens us. He calls us to do things that increase our satisfaction of heart.

If there is any area of your life that you are afraid to give to God, I encourage you to let it go. Let Him have whatever He wants. Let Him have whatever you are afraid to let Him have. Any place that you are unwilling to surrender to Him is a place where you are hardening your heart and blocking His life from flowing, and you are quenching the spirit and keeping yourself oppressed. You are shooting yourself in the foot spiritually.

Surrender gets you a satisfied heart. Lack of surrender gets you perpetual frustration and lack of satisfaction and lack of understanding. In the Word, lack of understanding is always a heart issue; it is never an IQ issue.

Jesus said to the disciples,

"Why do you not understand?
Do you have a hardened heart?"

And Paul, writing to the Ephesians, talked about those who:

"walk, in the futility of their mind,
being darkened in their understanding,
excluded from the life of God,
because of the ignorance that is in them,
because of the hardness of their heart;"

Having a hardened heart will

"darken your understanding" and
"exclude you from the life of God."

God has got the goods.

He has what you want.

He has liberty.

He has freedom.

He has health.

He has an abundance for every good deed.

He has the desires of your heart fulfilled.

He has pure love.

But, if you don't trust Him, and don't want to let Him have your heart, you will harden your heart and "walk in the futility of your mind" (of the flesh). When you read what Jesus taught, if you are not willing to do God's will, you will rationalize those teachings and won't understand the life-giving truth they contain, and you will harden your heart and miss the liberty Christ purchased for you. You just won't *get it.*

Surrender (being willing to do God's will) is foundational for recognizing truth and understanding it. The Bible records these statements:

"Purify your hearts, you double-minded."

"Keep the heart with all diligence,
for out of it flow the issues of life."

"Do you not understand? Do you have a hardened heart?"

Understanding the Gospel of Jesus Christ is a heart issue, not a head issue, and it is a simple Gospel. Gospel means good news. It is GOOD news, not bad news, and it is simple. A childlike heart of trust is the key to understanding. It is not about IQ; it is about having a tender heart.

You are not your flesh, but you are responsible for your flesh. You are expected to take steps to walk in what God says is real, rather than what your flesh feels is real. God says surrender is required to attain the freedom you desire. Your flesh says surrender will make you unhappy. Choose to believe the truth and reject the lie.

I chose to surrender when I was 25. I said,

"I want whatever You want, wherever You want it, for whatever reason you want it, with whoever you want it."

I gave Him all of my heart, and He flooded me with His astonishing love. I walked around in a cloud of love for days. I was with a group of friends, and one of them hugged me; then she gasped and pushed me away from her and asked me, "Can you feel that?" I said, "Yes," smiling, "I can feel that." She then passed me around and made about four other people hug me, one at a time. Each one did the same thing. With their hands on my upper arms, they would step back from me, and look at me with wide-eyed scrutiny. I'm not sure what they were feeling, but if they were feeling one tenth of the Presence of God that I felt, it was good.

God is real, and He is pure love. If you give Him your heart, He will give you His, and it is more lovely than words can say. Don't let the lie steal this life-liberating truth from you.

Surrender

Message Fifteen

Whatever YOU Desire

Therefore I say unto you, "What things soever ye desire, when ye pray, believe that ye receive them, and ye shall have them."

Mark 11:24

I'm not a big fan of the King James Version of the Bible, simply because I prefer more modern speech. With this particular verse, however, the KJV translation is just better than any others. Still, you can modernize it without losing the truth it contains, which is:

Whatever things *you desire*, when you pray, believe you receive them and you will.

This is a powerful truth! You *can* desire, pray, believe and receive.

Now listen. You can't desire and ask for crazy stuff like someone else's spouse. You *can,* however, desire and ask for any promise of God. Since healing is a promise of God, you certainly can include it in a legitimate list of *whatsoever things* you *can* desire, and you *can* have.

Regarding this Jesus tried to tell us that the sky's the limit. Look at these two verses.

Verse 22-23:

"And Jesus answering saith unto them, 'Have faith in God' (some translations say, 'Have the Faith of God'). For verily I say unto you, That whosoever shall say unto this mountain, 'be thou removed, and cast into the sea,' and shall not doubt in his heart, but shall believe that those things which he saith shall come to pass, he shall have whatsoever he saith."

Whatever you can believe for (all the way up to tossing a mountain into the sea) can be yours. Do you see that? Do you see He is saying, "*Hey, the sky is the limit. Don't be timid in your faith.*" They were all amazed because He cursed a fig tree, and it withered. He acts like it is no big deal and says you can toss a mountain into the sea if you have the faith for it.

The truth is that you are not going to have faith for anything that is not legally yours. If you have faith for it, then it is something that you can have. *Go for it!* Faith is confidence in truth. Faith cannot believe for something that is untruth. So if you have faith that you can change the weather, then that means changing the weather is something that belongs to you, or you would not have the faith for it.

Do you get that?

Okay, so physical healing . . . We know it is God's will, so we can have confidence that we are not asking for something we should not have. If we desire it, we can have it. *What things soever ye desire, when ye pray, believe that ye receive them, and ye shall have them.*

There are TWO keys:

1) Believe you have received it, *before* you have it.

2) SAY it.

Read these again:

> "For verily I say unto you, that whosoever shall SAY unto this mountain, 'be thou removed, and cast into the sea,' and shall not doubt in his heart, but shall believe that those things which he SAITH shall come to pass, he shall have whatsoever he SAITH."

You need to **speak** your prayer into the spiritual atmosphere around you.

"Death and life are in the power of the tongue, and he who is wise will eat the fruit thereof." Proverbs 18:21

"As you have spoken in My hearing, so I will do." Numbers 14:28

Speaking God's Word releases the anointing/power of God. Speak the Word over your life. Say it out loud. Release the Word to work in your life by speaking your requests or demands.

Demands?? Yes.

The Greek in the scripture where Jesus says, "Whatever you *ask* in My Name, that will I do," actually says, "Whatever you *demand* in My Name that I will do." Go over to Acts and watch Peter say to the crippled man, "Silver and gold have I none, but what I do have I give unto you, In the name of Jesus of Nazareth. Rise and walk!" He didn't supplicate; he commanded or demanded.

He didn't say, "Oh Dear Jesus, if it be Your will, would You please heal this poor crippled man? I know he is a filthy sinner and doesn't deserve it, but Lord he has suffered so much, we just need You to have mercy on him and touch him." Sound familiar? That kind of prayer is totally non-scriptural, and is based on disappointing life experiences, resulting from lack of knowledge, but is common in churches around the world.

Jesus really and truly said,

"Whatever you command in My name,
that will I do!"

You are not pointing your finger at God and demanding Him to act. You are pointing your finger at the situation and requiring it to change through the authority you have in Christ. There is just as much power in the name of Jesus as there was in Jesus when He walked the earth. Command sickness to go, just like He did, and it will.

If you see yourself as a terrible, hopeless sinner, rather than the righteousness of God in Christ Jesus, then you will not have the courage to desire, or believe, or demand/command. You have to look into the mirror of the Word, see yourself as what the Word says you are, ignore your flesh, and act like you believe God. When you do, you will be amazed. It will work, and your joy will be made full.

Whatever you have to do to get to the place where you believe what the Word says about you, you need to do it, and make haste to do it. Every day that you walk believing your flesh is the real you, you allow the enemy to steal your inheritance in Christ.

You are forgiven.

You are blessed.

You are not cursed.

You are loved.

Healing belongs to you.

Jesus bore your sins so that you
could be the righteousness of God.

Jesus bore your sickness
so that you could be healed.

Jesus is the will of God in action.

Jesus healed all who came to Him.

Whatever you desire you can have.

God is not withholding.

All things are possible to him who believes.

Desire it.

Say/ask/demand/command it.

Believe you receive it, before you see it.

Praise God for the answer, before you see it,

and you shall receive it.

Message Sixteen

Take Care How You Listen

I don't know about you, but I love the way Jesus taught. He really kept things simple. Nevertheless, what He taught is spiritually understood. It requires revelation to understand simple spiritual truth.

I mentioned earlier that I thought it was a good idea to pray the prayer that Paul prayed in Ephesians, asking for "a spirit of wisdom and revelation of the true knowledge of Jesus Christ." In my experience, it works folks. God actually answers that prayer and helps you to *see*. It is also good to know that you can take steps on your own to *hear* better.

In Luke 8, Jesus said,

'Take care how you listen; for whoever has, to him shall more be given; and whoever does not have, even what he thinks he has (seems to have) shall be taken away from him.'

This was spoken on the heels of Him teaching on the sower sowing the seed. Let's look at those scriptures as they give some insight into how to, "Take care how you listen."

Starting in verse 5:

"The sower went out to sow his seed; and as he sowed, some fell beside the road; and it was trampled under foot, and the birds of the air ate it up.

"And other seed fell on rocky soil, and as soon as it grew up, it withered away, because it had no moisture.

And other seed fell among the thorns; and the thorns grew up with it, and choked it out.

"And other seed fell into the good soil, and grew up, and produced a crop a hundred times as great. As He said these things, He would call out,

'He who has ears to hear, let him hear.'
"And the disciples began questioning Him as to what this parable might be.

"And He said, 'To you it has been granted to know the mysteries of the kingdom of God, but to the rest it is in parables, in order that Seeing they may not see, and hearing they may not understand.'

"Now the parable is this: the seed is the word of God.

"And those beside the road are those who have heard; then the devil comes and takes away the word from their heart, so that they may not believe and be saved.

"And those on the rocky soil are those who, when they hear, receive the word with joy; and these have no firm root; they believe for a while, and in time of temptation fall away.

"And the seed which fell among the thorns, these are the ones who have heard, and as they go on their way they are choked with worries and riches and pleasures of this life, and bring no fruit to maturity.

"And the seed in the good soil, these are the ones who have heard the word in an honest and good heart, and hold it fast, and bear fruit with perseverance.

"Now no one after lighting a lamp covers it over with a container, or puts it under a bed; but he puts it on a lamp stand, in order that those who come in may see the light.

"For nothing is hidden that shall not become evident, nor anything secret that shall not be known and come to light.

"Therefore take care how you listen for whoever has, to him shall more be given; and whoever does not have, even what he thinks he has shall be taken away from him."

If you are one of those people who skip over the scripture to get to the writing below it, don't do that. Go ahead and read the verses. The word of God is living and gives you life. Don't short change yourself and block the life available to you by not reading them.

He is saying that a lot of things can interfere with *getting it*. Life in general (both the good and the bad), can distract or discourage us, and cause us to not *see* or *hear* what the Word says. The good news is that we can make an effort to have an honest and good heart, and hold tightly to the Word, and persevere in that truth. The result is that the Word will bear fruit in our lives. We just need to take care how we listen. The ball is in our court, so to speak. The Word (Truth) of God is out there; our part is to respond appropriately to it.

We are talking Kingdom of God reality here. We have been transferred from the kingdom of darkness to the Kingdom of Light. We can enter in with gusto and learn the ways of this Kingdom and *see* deeply if we choose to.

Here is another simple, yet powerful teaching by Jesus on this subject.

Matthew 13:44:

"The kingdom of heaven is like a treasure hidden in the field, which a man found and hid; and from joy over it he goes and sells all that he has, and buys that field.

"Again, the kingdom of heaven is like a merchant seeking fine pearls, and upon finding one pearl of great value, he went and sold all that he had, and bought it."

If you really get it that His Words are the very life of your spirit, then you will eagerly pursue them. If you really believe that He has transferred you to the Kingdom of Light, you will want to break through the murky waters of your flesh into the fresh air of the spirit.

It is easy to be dull of hearing. Just trying to survive illness can make you so fatigued emotionally that it seems too challenging to try to wake up spiritually. But, waking up spiritually is necessary, so you want to make any effort you can to do so. Just take tiny steps, and, as you do it will start to flow; you will start to get energized, and your emotional fatigue will pass.

Jesus said to take care how you listen, because whoever has will be given more. It is wise to pay attention to that and know that as you take baby steps to know and act on truth, you will begin to wake up, and more truth will be added to you. And more truth equals more freedom.

There is a Bible proverb that says,

The path of the righteous is like the light of the dawn,
shining brighter and brighter until the full day.

Truth is like that in our lives. As we take those small steps to walk in the light, our light increases until eventually the sun is fully shining; so be encouraged. Take those small steps and watch your light increase. Don't stress over what you can't see. As you go, your light will increase, and it will be easier to see.

As Americans, it sure is easy to be lukewarm. Our hardest day would seem like a joyous relief to many of the world's population. Regular meals, safe homes, water coming out of pipes in the wall, beds to sleep on, good roads and predictable traffic—all these make it easy to be so full that we are not hungry for God. But we can stir ourselves up and pursue Kingdom knowledge with the fervor of the man who found a treasure in the field and sold all that he had to purchase the field. We can choose to increase the light in our lives.

One more Jesus teaching, and then I will quit.

Luke 11:33-34:

"No one, after lighting a lamp, puts it away in a cellar, nor under a peck measure (large basket), but on the lamp stand, in order that those who enter my see the light.

"The lamp of your body is your eye; (Greek idiom meaning "soul") when your eye is clear (single), your whole body also is full of light; but when it is bad, your body also is full of darkness.

"Then watch out that the light in you may not be darkness.

"If, therefore, your whole body is full of light, with no dark part in it, it shall be wholly illumined, as when the lamp illumines you with its rays."

We can be full of the light of God, and it is our choice. In fact, in our spirits we are already full of the light of God but our soul/flesh mind can be full of darkness that blocks the light. Nevertheless, as we take steps to be single-minded and to walk in the mind of Christ, it will transform our flesh and body, and we will be increasingly filled with the light of life. That is where I am going.

Paul's eye was single, and they carried handkerchiefs from his body to the sick and they were healed. Not only are we supposed to be healed, but we are supposed to be laying hands on the sick, so they recover.

I want to be awake. I want my eye to be single so that my body is full of light. I want to walk in the light as He is in the light. Jesus says I can, so I'm going to do all I can to be filled with light. I'm going to see myself as the Word says I am, and not let the enemy make me feel condemned.

Anybody with me here?

Take Care How You Listen

Message Seventeen

God Always Loves You

*L*ast night I had an amazing experience. I was watching a program showing a Christian meeting in Trinidad (West Indies). There was an 11-year-old girl who came up to tell about her experience while sitting in the congregation. She had sickle cell anemia and was there with her parents. With great emotion, she reported that while she was listening to the message she felt someone touch her. She asked her brother next to her if he had touched her, and he said no.

She went on to say that when she felt someone touch her, she also felt electric power go through her body, and she believed she was healed. She was so sweet. As the program progressed the power of God got all over her; she was shaking and visibly having a God encounter.

As the minister prayed for her to become an ambassador for Christ, she told him she had something to say. He gladly handed her the microphone, as it was obvious that God was doing something through her. She took the microphone and began to preach in the spirit. It was lovelier than I can say. She was shaking intensely and had to hold the microphone with two hands as she spoke boldly and passionately, mostly with her eyes closed.

I videotaped it and then transcribed it. It was so simple and yet so powerful; I thought I would share it with you. I wish you could have seen her and heard her tone; it was breathtaking. Her name is Philomena, and this is what she said, impassioned by the Spirit of God:

Everybody who doesn't believe in God–Believe in Him, and expect your miracle, because you never know what is going to happen.

When I was 9 (she is 11 now), I always prayed to God to show me a sign so that I could do His work. But I never believed anything like this! (Referring to being touched and healed.)

Even though you have a sickness, continue believing Jesus came on the earth and died for you, and He's still alive and that's the only thing. That's the only thing. Then you are saved, and when you are saved, the gift of Heaven is for you!

Did you know that the devil deceives you?

Because if you believe in God, that is all you have to believe.

Some people may be in trouble, and they are always like, *"God never helps me!"*

He does!

He has a way out of everything; you just have to look for it.

God says that you should not let the devil come over you! Because if you don't, He's not happy. [In other words: If you don't resist the devil, God is not happy]

And we are an example of Him. He's using us to reach other people, and everybody will be healed from anything they have, just by believing and having faith.

God always loves you!

And even though you make sin, just go and ask that, "God forgive me. I accept (responsibility) for what I did." And God is gonna forgive you, and you're gonna be one of His children.

If you need to learn anything, go to the Bible. That is the only thing that you can learn from (about God).

Every time, pray to God anywhere you are! Even if you're studying in school, just always keep your mind on God.

Pray!
Pray to God!
Don't ever stop praying to God!
Because God is your life and your strength!

When you give God your body!
Your life!
Your strength!
Your soul!
Your mind!
Your brain!
Your breath!
Your feet!
Your body!
Everything is possible!

Everything is possible!

Because there's nothing that is not possible when Jesus is here.

Jesus is always here!
Jesus is always here!

She was so impassioned, and It was such a rich God moment that I watched it three times and then read it and re-read it. My hope is that it will inspire you also, and you will agree that God always loves you, and with Him, all things are possible.

This is a new season folks. You may have walked with the Lord a long time and found that He didn't sprinkle magic dust on your life, making everything wonderful. Perhaps, even though you know Christ, your life has been hard. I want to encourage you regarding the reality that this is a new season. God is moving powerfully in our generation. He is turning up the volume, so to speak, and it is a time to reach up one more time because He is responding in new ways.

God Always Loves You

Message Eighteen

Thorn in The Flesh
Part 1

*R*ecently I had a phone conversation with someone who had some doubt about the idea of God wanting everyone to be healed. His doubts were based on Paul's "thorn in the flesh." He mentioned the letter Paul wrote to the Corinthians where he talks about being given a *thorn in the flesh*. I'm figuring others have similar questions, so let's talk about it.

2 Corinthians 12:7-10:

> "And because of the surpassing greatness of the revelations, for this reason, to keep me from exalting myself, there was given me a thorn in the flesh, a messenger of Satan to buffet me—to keep me from exalting myself.

> "Concerning this I entreated the Lord three times that it might depart from me.

> "And He said to me, 'My grace is sufficient for you, for power is perfected in weakness.' Most gladly, therefore, I will rather boast about my weaknesses, that the power of Christ may dwell in me.

> "Therefore I am well content with weaknesses, with insults, with distresses, with persecutions, with difficulties, for Christ's sake; for when I am weak, then I am strong."

Apparently a multitude of Bible teachers have taught that Paul's thorn in the flesh was an incurable physical ailment, which he prayed about three times, without success. God didn't heal him.

When I found these verses back in the early eighties, I wondered what *thorn in the flesh* meant. It sounded like a figure of speech to me—sort of like our modern "pain in the neck." I didn't own a book that had Jewish figures of speech, so I thought to myself, "I wonder if this term was used in the Old Testament, or elsewhere in the New Testament?"

I got my trusty concordance out and looked up all the references to "thorn" that I could find. I narrowed those down to: "thorn in the flesh" or "thorn in the side", etc. What I found was that this always referred to an enemy that was harassing you. Not once did it ever refer to an illness. It seems to be a Jewish figure of speech that means verbal harassment by an enemy.

There is zero reason to believe (based on these verses) that Paul had an incurable illness for which he prayed for, for relief, and God didn't heal him. He clearly states his *thorn in the flesh* was a messenger of Satan. He goes on to talk about insults, distresses, difficulties and persecutions. Someone obviously was harassing Paul, and God told Him that His Grace was sufficient for power is perfected in weakness. Well, to me that means God was saying, *I can give you Grace in this situation so that it won't even bother you. You can have joy even though harassed.* That concept makes sense to me since Paul taught that God always causes us to triumph in Christ.

Paul does mention, elsewhere in his writings, that he preached to a specific group because of a weakness of the flesh, and they welcomed him like an angel of the Lord, and would have plucked out their eyes and given them to him if they could have. Some have taken this to mean that he had some incurable eye disease. A close look at the scriptures, however, shows that this weakness of the flesh/eye issue happened after he had been stoned and left for dead. Those who were with him stood around him, and he got up and went into the city to preach. I suspect he actually was dead, and they raised him up.

You can imagine what a person's face would look like if they had been stoned just a few hours before. When stoning someone, the head is the main target. Undoubtedly, his face and eyes were swollen and bruised, and probably even bloody, and I'm sure that people felt compassion for him and wished they could help him. This seems like a much more likely reason for him to say they wanted to pluck their own eyes out and give them to him, if it were possible; rather than thinking that the man who had such a healing anointing that they carried cloths from his body to heal the sick, had an incurable eye disease.

Anytime you come across a scripture that doesn't make sense to you, it is a good idea to get a concordance and see if you can find more information about it. There are also books out there that can help, like books on Jewish figures of speech, but sometimes just running through the notes in the columns is helpful.

Here's one example I enjoy: Matthew 5 Jesus said,

"Blessed are the meek (or humble) for they shall inherit the earth."

Do you know what that verse means? For the longest time, I didn't. Though I read my Bible daily, it was thirty years before I figured it out. Once I did, I surveyed a number of my Christian friends, and not one of them knew what it meant. They all had half-baked ideas like I did. I had a back-of-the-mind thought about what it meant. But mostly it just didn't make sense to me. Then one day, after praying for God's opinion on prosperity, I was reading Psalm 37 and found this same verse, and realized that Jesus was quoting scripture that He knew his contemporaries would recognize, and He knew they would fill in the remainder of the passage in their minds.

Here is the full quote:

Psalm 37:11:

But the humble ("meek" in KJV) will inherit the land,
And will delight themselves in abundant prosperity.

End quote.

Oh my goodness; what a completely different picture! I already knew by doing a word search that you humble yourself by being obedient to God. So, essentially, this verse says those who are smart enough to do things God's way will inherit the land and delight themselves in abundant prosperity. Far from saying poor, earthy people can console themselves with the fact that they at least get to farm the land, it says they will own land and prosper abundantly.

No one that I surveyed had any idea that this verse meant anything like this. So then I go back to Matthew 5 and check the references in the column, and right there is a reference to Psalm 37:11. Insert rolling eyes here. I could have had this bit of revelation thirty years earlier if I had just read the reference in the column. So it pays to look beyond the surface when you come upon something in the Word that doesn't make sense to you.

Truth sets people free; misinterpretation of the truth keeps people in bondage. Paul's *thorn in the flesh* was not an incurable illness, so don't let the enemy use those verses to dampen your faith that God wants you well.

Remember that Jesus healed all who came to Him.

Remember that Jesus said,

"I came not to do my own will
but that of the Father."

Remember that Jesus is God's will in action.

Remember that Jesus is the same,
"Yesterday, today and forever."

Choose to believe that Jesus still
heals all who come to Him.

Choose to believe that it is still God's will
to heal all who come to Him.

Choose to believe that
you are supposed to be well,
and that you are supposed to be
laying hands on the sick,
so that they recover.

Choose to line your mind up with your heart.

In your heart, you know that God is love,
and that Love wants you well.

Note: Regarding Psalm 37:11, not all translations say abundant prosperity. NAS does. The word translated "prosperity" is actually Shalom, which has a very deep meaning. It can be translated health, peace, or prosperity. Shalom actually means total healing of your entire life. When an Israelite says Shalom to someone, they are declaring total provision for them in every part of their life. It is not simply a social greeting; it is a power-filled blessing.

In addition, I am confident that the Lord led me to this, and made it obvious to me, for a reason. I had just prayed, *Please show me your opinion on prosperity,* and then I saw this in the NAS, which translates it as abundant prosperity.

It is my understanding that shalom means, *"May all the blessings of the covenant be yours."* That would certainly include prosperity.

Message Nineteen

Healing Is For All Believers

Question: Does God want to heal all believers?
Answer: Yes; of *all* diseases.

References:

Matthew 4:23-24:

> "And Jesus was going about in all Galilee, teaching in their synagogues, and proclaiming the gospel of the kingdom, and healing every kind of disease and every kind of sickness among the people.
>
> And the news about Him went out into all Syria, and they brought to Him ALL WHO WERE ILL, taken with various diseases and pains, demoniacs, epileptics, paralytics; and He healed them."

Matthew 9:35:

> "And Jesus was going about all the cities and the villages, teaching in their synagogues, and proclaiming the gospel of the kingdom, and healing every kind of disease and every kind of sickness."

*R*eally hear that. He was proclaiming the gospel of the Kingdom. He was proclaiming the good news that there is a Kingdom of Light that we can live in, in which healing is ours, prosperity is ours, and eternal life is ours. This is indeed good news, which He backed up with power. He healed *every* kind of sickness and disease.

Matthew 12:15:

"But Jesus aware of this, withdrew from there. And many followed Him, and He HEALED THEM ALL."

Matthew 14:14:

"And when He went ashore, He saw a great multitude, and felt compassion for them, and healed their sick."

It doesn't say He healed some of their sick. It says He healed their sick.

Matthew 14:34-36:

And when they had crossed over, they came to land at Gennesaret. And when the men of that place recognized Him, they sent into all the surrounding district and brought to Him ALL WHO WERE SICK; and they began to entreat Him that they might just touch the fringe of His cloak; and AS MANY AS TOUCHED IT WERE CURED.

Luke 6 17-19:

"And He descended with them, and stood on a level place, and there was a great multitude of His disciples, and a great throng of people from all Judea and Jerusalem and the coastal region of Tyre and Sidon who had come to hear Him, and to be healed of their diseases; and those who were troubled with unclean spirits were being cured.

And all the multitude were trying to touch Him, for power was coming from Him and HEALING THEM ALL."
(Emphasis mine, in all verses above.)

All these verses report that Jesus healed ALL who came to Him. There is not one verse in the Bible that says He sent someone away without healing them. He was moved with compassion and healed ALL who came to Him.

There is so much to say about that. Just His compassion alone should give us confidence. Pick up a concordance and check out the references on compassion, and you will see God's loving, compassionate nature. That will strengthen your faith. But did Jesus only heal out of compassion? I don't think so. I think He healed because it is God's will.

If you go back to Deuteronomy, and read about the Old Covenant, you will see that sickness is a result of the curse. The curse occurs when we reject God. The New Testament/New Covenant says that Christ redeemed us from the curse of the law (old covenant). When I read Deuteronomy 28, and it lists sickness as part of the curse, I logically conclude that Jesus redeemed me from sickness.

Jesus, the sinless one, died on the cross. Though He was sinless, He became our substitute and died the death of a criminal so that we could be free from the punishment due us as spiritual criminals. He became sin so that we could become the righteousness of God.

The curse came about because of sin,
and sickness came about because of the curse.

No sin, no curse.
No curse, no sickness.

Does that mean you have to be sinless to be free of the curse? No. It means you accept Jesus as your substitute, and you get declared sin-free and, therefore, curse-free.

Being sin-free is something that Jesus purchased for everyone, and being healed is also something He purchased for everyone. You cannot separate the two, and the Jews He was speaking to knew that. They knew the Old Testament very well, having memorized it by the time they were thirteen. They knew that if they were declared sin-free, they had a right to healing. He didn't have to explain that to them. It was Jewish common knowledge that "freedom from sin" and "healing" go hand in hand. That is why Jesus said to the paralytic (and to me,) "Your sins are forgiven." When your sins are forgiven, you have the right to be healed.

If your sins are forgiven, there is only one thing that can stand between you and healing: lack of knowledge. If you really understand that sickness is a result of the curse of the Law, and that Jesus has redeemed you from that curse, then you will know that sickness has no legal right to stay in your body. Not because you are perfect, but because you are forgiven.

Healing is for everyone; just as being born again and transferred from the kingdom of darkness to the Kingdom of Light is for everyone. Does that mean that everyone is saved and born again? No, only those who accept it and receive it. Does that mean that everyone is healed? Unfortunately, no; only those who accept it and receive it.

Jesus healed ALL who came to Him
of ALL their diseases and sicknesses.

Anyone who has experienced forgiveness (and is reborn spiritually through Jesus Christ), has the right to be healed. Anyone who has not experienced forgiveness (and is not reborn spiritually through Jesus), can also be healed through prayer. Remember that no one Jesus healed was born-again.

EVERYONE CAN BE SAVED,
AND EVERYONE CAN BE HEALED.

Bless the Lord oh my soul and forget not all His benefits.
He forgives all my sins and heals all my diseases.
—Psalm 103

Healing is not for a select few.
It is not for those who are especially worthy.

Jesus didn't take people's spiritual inventory
unless they were rejecting Him.

Even under the old covenant,
people were forgiven of their sins
in order to receive healing.

Jesus forgave all and healed all.

He never sent anyone away,
telling them it was not God's will for them to be healed.

He never sent anyone away saying that
God wanted them to be sick
so that they would grow up spiritually.

He never sent anyone away saying
it wasn't the right time for them to be healed.

He was moved with compassion,
and healed ALL who came to Him.

Jesus is moved by compassion
when He sees you suffering.

He is the vine, and you are the branch.

He is not far away out in space.
He is close.

He is one with you.

He is acutely aware of you.

His compassion is stirred toward you.

He wants you well.

Enjoy that truth.

Thank Him that He healed all who came to Him.

Thank Him that He still heals all who come to Him.

Don't let the enemy cancel your faith
with pictures of those who were not healed.

Even if others didn't get healed, *YOU CAN.*
Even if you prayed before and didn't get healed,
it doesn't mean you can't get healed now.

Faith is confidence in God's integrity.

Faith is confidence in God's compassion.

Faith is confidence in God's forgiveness.

Faith is confidence in God's nearness.

God is love.

He loves you.

He forgives you.

He is not mad at you.

His steadfast love never ceases.

He radiates love like the sun radiates light.

God always loves you.

Rest in that.

Embrace it.

Let it fill your heart.

Let it feed your faith.

Healing is for everyone!

Go back over the preceding statements and tap while you declare them over yourself. Change them enough to make them personal.

Examples:

God loves me,
He is not mad at me,
He forgives me,
He wants me to be well.

Tap on the EFT acupoints while you declare each truth, and notice how those statements seem more real to you. As I said before, tapping while declaring the truth allows the truth to come alive in your heart more easily. It seems to weaken the flesh's ability to block truth.

Message Twenty

Thorn in The Flesh
Part 2

I was thinking about how we can see a multitude of verses in the Word which clearly state God is compassionate and wants to heal the sick, but if we see maybe three verses that *seem* to say that is not true, we will instantly dump all our faith (built on an enormous amount of scripture), in order to embrace the idea that He doesn't want everyone well, simply because our experience agrees with the lie and we believe that, instead of believing the truth.

With that in mind, I'd like to challenge you to do something I have done. Get some notebook paper and a cheap notebook (or an expensive one if you want) and search out, and write down, any scripture you can find that is pro "God wants me well.". Also, write down all the ones you can find that seem to disagree. You will find this to be a wonderful faith-building exercise as you see many, many *clear* verses that say God wants you well, and struggle to find any verses that *clearly* say He does not want you well.

Ask Jesus to open up the Word to you. I mentioned a couple of times now that you can pray like Paul, and ask for a spirit of wisdom and revelation in the true knowledge of Jesus Christ. I frequently pray that in faith, believing I will receive.

Believe you receive.

This is a good place to begin to practice believing you receive. Believe you receive revelation knowledge regarding God's heart in the area of healing and health.

Considering the misconception that Paul was sick and prayed three times, but God wouldn't heal him, I was reading 2 Corinthians 11, where Paul lists the things he had suffered as a servant of Christ. I will list them here.

Verse 23:

Far more labors
Far more imprisonments
Five times I received 39 lashes from the Jews
Three times I was beaten with rods
Once I was stoned
Three times I was shipwrecked
Spent a night and a day in the deep
Frequent journeys
In dangers from rivers
Dangers from my countrymen
Dangers from the Gentiles
Dangers in the city
Dangers in the wilderness
Dangers on the sea
Dangers among false brethren
In labor and hardship
Through many sleepless nights
In hunger and thirst
Often without food
In cold and exposure
Let down in a basket through a window in the wall

He goes into a great deal of detail about what he has suffered as a servant of Christ. Personally, I think that if he ever had a serious incurable illness while serving Christ, he would have clearly said so. Furthermore, I think he would have taught, extensively, that believers should embrace illness as a means of spiritual growth. He never, ever taught anything like that.

He went around preaching the Kingdom of God is here, and backing up what he preached with power. He healed for the same reasons Christ did, to show that this is God's will and the normal manner of life for those who live in His Kingdom.

Paul was used mightily by God and had an incredible healing ministry. Handkerchiefs were carried from his body to heal the sick. He radiated the power of God. Can you see how illogical it is to think that a sick man, with oozing puss-filled eyes (as some people teach, though it is nowhere in the Word) would be an inspiration to others to believe he could heal them? It isn't logical.

Saturate yourself in the Word, which says God wants you well, and set aside the few profoundly unclear statements that *might* seem to say that He doesn't. Let faith arise in your heart. Meditate on the simple truth that Jesus is God's will in action, and He was moved with compassion and healed ALL who came to Him. With a sincere heart, spend some time meditating on that—perhaps thanking God for that reality—and see if you start to feel the compassion of God toward you.

Let it grow, and enjoy it.

You are being transformed by
the renewing of your mind.

Your eye is becoming single.

The light in you is increasing.

Your dawn is turning
into the light of the full day.

Embrace it and have faith in it.

Message Twenty-One

Redeemed from
the Curse of the Law

*T*oday I want to share a little about what it means to be "redeemed from the curse of the law." If you remember, part of my prayer was, "I am redeemed from the curse and, therefore, sickness has no legal right to be in my body." What does it mean to be "redeemed from the curse of the law"?

As our covenant partner, God said He would be our healer. The word "healer" is Jehova-Rapha, which means: "I am the Lord that heals you", or, "I am the Lord your physician", or, "the self-existent One who reveals Himself as your healer or physician."

In Exodus 23:15 and Deuteronomy 7:15, He basically said that if we walked with Him in simple childlike obedience, He would be our healer. He would take sickness out of the midst of us and we would experience covenant blessings of all kinds; including freedom from illness. If we rejected Him as God (our Provider), we would reject a covenant relationship with Him, and we would be subject to the curse of the Law.

You can read Deuteronomy, where He went into great detail about this covenant. The blessings came from obedience to Him; the curse came from rejecting Him. Not because He required belief in Him, or He would get ticked off and make life miserable for us, but because He is the source of all life, and only by sticking close to Him and trusting in His wisdom and following His guidance, could we enjoy His supernatural safe-keeping and provision. Both the blessings and the curses are detailed in Deuteronomy 28, so that there would be no confusion about what a blessing is and what a curse is. The blessing came by being connected to the Life of God, and the curse came from disconnecting from His Life and His power to provide. If you turn off the lights, you get darkness. It is not an emotional issue. It is just a fact. Separate yourself from God, who is Light and Life and Love, and you get lack of Light and Life and Love, which results in sickness, lack, loneliness, fear, etc.

Here is a list of the diseases that Moses states would come upon those who broke covenant with God, allowing the curse to come upon themselves:

> Consumptions
> Fever
> Inflammation
> Fiery heat
> Blight
> Mildew
> Boils from the toes to the top of head
> Tumors
> Scab
> Itch
> Madness
> Blindness
> Bewilderment of heart
> Extraordinary plagues
> Severe and lasting plagues
> Miserable and chronic sickness
> All diseases . . . of which you are afraid, and
> Every sickness and every plague, which is not written in the book of this law.

This is not an unclear picture. Sickness is a result of the curse.

What about the Blessings?

Deuteronomy 4:30:

> "When you are in distress and all these things have come upon you, in the latter days, you will return to the Lord your God and listen to His voice.

31 For the Lord your God is a compassionate God; He will not fail you nor destroy you nor forget the covenant with your fathers which He swore to them."

(Back to 29) "But from there you will seek the Lord your God, and you will find Him if you search for Him with all your heart and all your soul."

Let's read the definition of compassion before we go on.

Compassion: Sympathetic consciousness of the distress of others, together with a desire to alleviate it.

That's who God is. He is not mad at you, and He is not withholding. He hasn't moved. He is waiting for us to move in His direction. He has what we want. It's our move. If we seek Him with our whole heart, mind, soul, and strength, He promises we will find Him, and we will find Him compassionate.

Let's go to Deuteronomy 7:15:

"And the Lord will remove from you all sickness; and He will not allow on you any of the harmful diseases of Egypt which you have known . . ."

Some translations say He will not "put" any disease on you, but it is my understanding that, in the original Hebrew, the word has a permissive tense and should read, "allow".

Deuteronomy 29:29 says:

"The secret things belong to the Lord our God, but the things revealed belong to us and our children forever, that we may observe all the words of this law."

There's a lot we can't figure out about spiritual reality, yet there are some things we don't need to know. For instance, I don't need to know how I will travel to heaven when I leave my body; I can relax and leave it to God. What I need to know, however, so that I can cooperate with Him and be blessed, He has revealed.

He has revealed that He is compassionate and wants to help us. If we will trust Him with childlike obedience, He will be God to us and will heal us.

Later in Deuteronomy 30:19-20 Moses said,

"I call heaven and earth to witness against you today, that I have set before you life and death, the blessing and the curse. So choose life in order that you may live, you and your descendants, by loving the Lord your God, by obeying His voice and by holding fast to Him; for this is your life and the length of your days . . ."

That is a super-condensed version of the Old Covenant:

Before Christ, there was no spiritual restoration. Nevertheless, God was still able to take care of them physically if they yielded to Him. When prophets like Moses spoke, they spoke as the Spirit came upon them. He was not IN them. Then, a few thousand years later, Jesus the Christ comes on the scene. Okay, first of all, Christ is not His last name. Naturally speaking, His name would have been Yeshua bar Joseph, which in English is "Jesus, son of Joseph." "Christ" is Greek and means, "Anointed one." The Jewish, or Hebrew, word "Messiah" means the same.

What does "anointed" mean? From what I have studied, it means appointed and empowered. Jesus was appointed and empowered to reverse the curse, not only externally (in our physical realm), but also internally (in our spirit). That is what it means to be born again, or born from above.

Your spirit is restored when you accept Jesus—the appointed and empowered one—as your substitute. You become a New Creation in Christ and have the mind of Christ. When you are born again, you know it is real. You know you are different. People might look at you on the outside and think you look the same, but you know you are different.

Jesus came to reverse the curse of the Law, both internally, and externally. Galatians 3:13 says, *Christ has redeemed us from the curse of the law having become a curse for us.*

Webster's definition of redeem: To buy back: free from captivity by payment of ransom.

Remember that the Word says we have been transferred from the kingdom of darkness to the Kingdom of Light. That is what Jesus did. He redeemed us from the curse of the Law and transferred us from the curses to the blessings.

2 Corinthians 1:20 says:

"For as many as may be the promises of God, in Him (Jesus) they are yes; wherefore also in Him is our Amen to the glory of God through us."

Boy is that a mouthful. It means every promise in the Bible that you can find is yes in Jesus. It is ours because of what Jesus did, and because we are now one with Jesus. But it also says our Amen is in Jesus. What does that mean? Amen means "So be it," or "Let it be so in my life." So, when you pray and say "Amen," you are saying "Let it be so in my life." Jesus purchased your right to say "Let it be so in my life."

Let's go back to the Old Testament to Isaiah 53, the whole chapter:

1 "Who has believed our message? And to whom has the arm of the Lord been revealed?

2 For He grew up before him like a tender shoot, and like a root out of parched ground; He has no stately form or majesty that we should look upon Him, nor appearance that we should be attracted to Him.

3 He was despised and forsaken of men, a man of sorrows (pains) and acquainted with grief (sickness or disease); and like one from whom men hide their face, He was despised, and we did not esteem Him.

4 Surely our grief's (sickness) He Himself bore, and our sorrows (pains) He carried; yet we ourselves esteemed Him stricken, smitten of God, and afflicted.

5 But He was pierced through for our transgressions, He was crushed for our iniquities; the chastening for our well-being fell upon Him and by His scourging we are healed.

6 All of us like sheep have gone astray. Each of us has turned to his own way; but the Lord has caused the iniquity of us all to fall (encounter) on Him.

7 He was oppressed and he was afflicted, yet He did not open His mouth; like a lamb that is led to slaughter (a sacrificial lamb), and like a sheep that is silent before its shearers, so He did not open His mouth.

8 By oppression and judgment He was taken away; and as for His generation, who considered that He was cut off out of the land of the living, for the transgression of my people to whom the stroke was due?

9 His grave was assigned with wicked men, yet He was with a rich man in His death, because He had done no violence, nor was there any deceit in His mouth.

10 But the Lord was pleased to crush Him, putting Him to grief; if He would render Himself as a guilt offering. He will see His offspring, He will prolong His days, and the good pleasure of the Lord will prosper in His hand.

11 As a result of the anguish of His soul, He will see it and be satisfied; by His knowledge the righteous One, My Servant, will justify the many, as He will bear their iniquities.

12 Therefore, I will allot Him a portion with the great, and He will divide the booty with the strong; because He poured out Himself to death, and was numbered with the transgressors; yet He Himself bore the sin of many, and interceded for the transgressors.

This is one major prophecy given regarding Christ. It clearly says He was innocent and bore our sins and our sickness.

Now you might read that and say, "How do we know it refers to Jesus?" Well, let's jump forward to Matthew 8:16-17:

"And when evening had come, they brought to Him many who were demon-possessed, and He cast out the spirits with a word, and healed all who were ill in order that what was spoken through Isaiah the prophet might be fulfilled, saying, "He Himself took our infirmities and carried away our diseases.""

He's quoting Isaiah 53:4.

If you get your Bible and read that verse it will say *grief* and *sorrow,* so why did Matthew say *infirmities* and *diseases*? Well, because that is what it actually says in the Hebrew (and the column notes in my NAS Bible).

If you look up the words *grief* and *sorrow* in a Bible concordance, you will find that *pain* and *sickness* are correct translations, not *grief* or *sorrow*. You will also see that they are translated correctly as *pain* and *sickness* in many, many other places in the Old Testament. Personally, I think this is one place where the translators dropped the ball and translated the words incorrectly, according to their current level of revelation and, therefore, their personal doctrine.

We know the correct translation, because Matthew, quoting this scripture, clearly states that He was a man of PAIN and acquainted with SICKNESS . . . surely our SICKNESS He Himself bore and our PAIN He carried . . . by His scourging (or lashes of a whip) we are HEALED . . .

Remember Psalm 103:

"Praise the Lord O my soul and forget not all His benefits, Who forgives all my sins and heals all my diseases."

Heals all my diseases,
Heals all my diseases,
Heals all my diseases!

Jesus took your sin and your sickness.

He became sin so you could be
the righteousness of God in Him.

He became sick so you could be healed.

Sinners who reject the covenant are subject to the curse, but Jesus healed even these. Not one person that was healed by Christ was born-again or redeemed from the curse; nevertheless, Jesus healed all who came to Him. Certainly, if those who were under the Old Covenant could be healed, then those under the New Covenant can and should be healed.

If you have believed in, and put your trust in Christ, then you are in covenant with Him, and you are no longer a sinner, you are a saint. You are the righteousness of God in Christ Jesus, and sickness has no right to stay in your body—unless, you fail to exercise your Christ given rights.

One more scripture:

1 Peter 2:22-24:

> (Jesus) who committed no sin, nor was any deceit found in His mouth (Isaiah 53:9)
>
> and while being reviled, He did not revile in return; while suffering He uttered no threats, but kept entrusting Himself to Him who judges righteously;
>
> and He himself bore our sins in His body on the cross, that we might die to sin and live to righteousness; for by His wounds you were healed.

Don't interpret that other than literally. Don't decide it means you are healed spiritually, because it doesn't. We are not healed spiritually. We are born again, and are new creatures. As spirits, we were dead, but now we are alive. That is not healing; it is restoration.

In summary:

Jesus redeemed us from the curse of the law, having become a curse for us. He bore the sickness and the pain due to us under the curse. Our sins are forgiven and we cannot be punished with the curse of the law unless we lie down and let the enemy work. We can be free from the curse of the law if we take hold of our rights in our heart, and insist that the enemy cease and desist.

I know this has been long, but in order for you to understand the prayer I prayed, you have to understand that sickness has no legal right to be in your body. Your sins are forgiven and you are no longer under the enemy's dominion. You now have a legal right to claim all the benefits of the New Covenant. You now have a legal right to claim all the promises of God that Christ purchased for you.

ALL THE PROMISES OF GOD
ARE YES IN JESUS.

God is not holding anything against you. He sees you as righteous. He sees you as forgiven. Christ was punished so you could go free. Go rent the movie The Passion, and watch it, and let it sink in that Jesus suffered so you don't have to.

When you really believe that God's word is true, and that Jesus carried your sickness and pain, and you choose to *believe that you receive* the healing Christ purchased for you, you will be well. I highly recommend that you meditate on this truth until it goes off inside you and you get it.

Do EFT for the lies in your emotions that disagree with who the Word says you are. Take the necessary steps to become single-minded on this subject. You have the mind of Christ in your spirit. You also have the mind of your flesh. Which one you live out of is your choice. Choose by faith to let the mind of Christ dominate.

We walk by faith in the mind of Christ and the Work of Christ, and not by sight or symptoms.

Faith is a choice. If it weren't, Jesus would have been out of line for scolding the disciples for being fearful instead of having faith. Remember when they were in the boat in a storm, He said, "Where is your faith?" That would be a very unkind and unproductive statement if we had no ability to increase our own faith, or choose to have faith. The good news in that statement is that we *can* increase our faith. We *can* respond differently. We *can* choose to have great faith. Meditating on the truth I have shared here will increase your faith.

Jesus is the Will of God in action.

Jesus healed ALL who came to Him.

Jesus is the same: yesterday, today and forever.

Jesus still heals all who come to Him.

Jesus said,
"All things are possible to the one who believes."

Jesus said,
"Whatever you pray believing you shall receive."

You can have more faith or less faith.
That is good news.

Saturate yourself with the truth that you can be well. This will increase your faith.

Choose to believe that God is compassionate and has made a way for you to be free of sin and sickness, and all the power of the enemy.

Tap on those truths.
Meditate on them.
Speak them over yourself.

Message Twenty-Two

EFT for Sickness

*H*ere is a long list of EFT phrases for eliminating emotions around sickness. Tapping on each of these will bring more balance into your body and will help your emotions line up with the Word regarding healing. I highly recommend doing any or all of these. The key is to connect with the emotion while tapping. Actually feel it. If you don't feel it, then it is not an issue for you and tapping would be a waste of time.

Comment: Some people I have coached are very reluctant to admit that they have any negative emotions, and are especially reluctant to say them out loud. There is so much teaching out there on the subject of "you get what you say" that people don't want to say what they feel, believing that it will only cement it in them. Fortunately, with EFT, that is not what happens. The opposite happens. Admitting your true feelings, while tapping on a few basic acupressure points, releases those emotions from you. On the other hand, when you refuse to acknowledge your true feelings you allow them to continue to affect you negatively.

The Bible does say that Death and Life are in the power of the tongue, but it is not talking about emotions. It is talking about your beliefs. Saying, "God is nowhere around," is very different from saying, "I **feel** like God is no where around." You can know in your belief system that God is near, and still feel in your emotions that He is nowhere around. God responds to what you believe. If you believe and say that you *will never get well*, then that is what you will get. But saying, "I *feel* like I'm un-fixable," is not the same as saying, "I b*elieve* I am un-fixable."

Admitting that you have flesh feelings that conflict with what you believe and tapping while doing so, will release those lies from you. Don't let profound freedom slip from you because you are afraid to be honest about your feelings. If you still feel like you are making a negative statement, and giving it negative power over you, put it in the past tense. Try, "I have felt", or "I have had the feeling . . . "

We can make positive statements and tap on them (and I recommend that), but I have noticed that positive statements are not as effective until we eliminate the negative emotions running around in the background. Once you have done enough EFT on the negative emotions, then the positive statements really start to work. This should not be surprising, or confusing. It is easy to understand that when you have less negative emotions lurking inside—disagreeing with your positive statement—then the positive statement will more readily find a home in your heart.

Also, don't expect one-minute wonders like you see posted on the EFT site: www.emofree.com. It can and does happen, however, chronic illness generally has deep emotional stuff attached to it and those lies come out one at a time. The good news is that every lie that leaves your emotions leaves you just a little freer, and better able to access your faith.

If you have read what the Word says about God wanting you well, and about Jesus purchasing your healing for you, then what is hindering you from receiving? I believe it is our natural emotions, which conflict with our faith.

What we feel negates what we believe.

When those lying emotions are gone, it's just you and the truth, and it becomes easy to receive. Do the work and you will see for yourself that this is true. Do as many of these statements as you feel like doing. Add to the list. If something comes up that is specific to you, you might want to write it down. I have noticed that once an emotion is gone, I actually forget that it ever existed. I mean . . . I could be in the shower and a lying emotion would come up, and I'd tap, and it would leave, and I'd think, *I will write that down when I get out of the shower.* Repeatedly, however, I have found I am completely unable to remember what the emotion was that I had tapped away. This is very common.

I've seen this happen with people I have coached. We will work on some deep stuff and it will leave them, and during the next session, when I talk about certain negative emotions they eliminated in the previous session, they actually have no memory that it was EVER a problem for them. It is quite remarkable. By writing down the issues you are eliminating, it will encourage you to look back and realize how many things just don't bother you anymore.

Try to do some each day, at least four to five days a week. You will see that you make remarkable progress.

The following are based on the basic EFT phrase:

"Even though I _____, I deeply and completely love and accept myself."

You can fill that blank with any of the statements below:

I feel sad that I'm sick
I feel sad (or angry or depressed) that I've been sick for ___ years (or months or days)
I hate being sick
I feel like a victim
I feel powerless to help myself
I'm afraid I'll never get well
Being sick makes me feel unloved
I feel like a powerless victim
I feel unloved
I feel like if God loved me, I'd be well
I feel incurable
I feel inferior because I'm ill
I feel like I'm being punished
I feel disappointed with God
I wish I were well right now
I desire perfect health
I feel like I'm in prison
I feel embarrassed that I'm not well
I wonder if I'm sick because _____
I wonder if it's emotionally based
Suffering makes me feel unloved
I don't know what to tap for to help myself

I don't know how to get well
I feel sad/bad/alone
I feel really hurt by my limitations
I feel *less than* because of my limitations
I feel powerless to fix my body
I feel hurt that God has not healed me
I feel like God doesn't love me or else He would heal me
I feel like I'm missing it somewhere or else God would heal me
I feel like something bad in me is blocking my healing
I feel like God is unhappy with me or else He would heal me
I feel sad that God still hasn't healed me
I feel sorry for myself because I'm still not well
I really resent not being well
I feel like God doesn't love me in this area
I feel like I can't get what I need from God
I feel angry that God hasn't healed me
I feel social pressure to be successful by being well
I feel hurt by physical limitations
I don't understand what is hampering me
I don't understand why I don't have faith for me to be well
I'm afraid if I ask Jesus to heal me, and He does, then He will
expect a lot from me
I feel like if I had health and wealth, it would make me a
cheater
I feel like I would have to cheat in order to have health
I feel like God wants me to suffer, so I make better choices
I feel angry because I don't want to suffer
I want all hindrances gone and want health now
I feel un-fixable
I feel angry at God that He allowed me to be sick for so long
and waste so much of my life
Total health seems foreign to me
I'm afraid I can't get well
I'm angry with myself for being emotionally weak and getting
sick
I feel like Jesus has let me down
I feel sad about years of life lost to sickness
I feel angry with myself for making bad health choices.
I feel like God only heals nice people, and I'm not nice enough
for Him to heal me
I feel like it's a waste of time to pray to be healed
I feel jealous of others who have gotten healed/well

Once you have eliminated a large portion of negative emotions like these, then you can start to do positive statements like those below.

Even though I'm struggling with my health today, I give myself permission to be well.

Even though I have prayed for instant healing before and it didn't happen, I choose to believe God will heal me instantly.

Even though I feel like there is some reason why God doesn't want to heal me, I choose to believe that that is a lie, and that the truth is that God does want to heal me.

Even though I feel like I'm unhealable, I choose to believe that I am heal-able and I choose to see myself well.

Other statements that have worked well for me are below. They *do not* include the normal,

"Even though I _____, I deeply and completely love and accept myself."

They are complete as they are. You can do one phrase on all your acupoints, or you can do one phrase on each acupoint. Start at the KC (Karate Chop point), and then go to the EB (eye brow) and so on.

(For a free graphic on the EFT points, scroll to the end of this chapter, or go to http://www.fol-hs.com)

KC: I want my body to repair whatever needs repairing so that I feel excellent, or have excellent health.

EB: I want to be free of all lies that hinder me from being well.

SE: I want my body to line-up with the Word of God and be healed.

UE: I want the truth about healing to set me free.

UN: I want faith to be healed.

Chin: I want all lies that hinder me to be gone.

CB: I want all emotional hindrances to my faith to be gone.

UA: I want to trust God to help me with all this.

KC: I want to believe God loves me and wants me to be well.

You can also do positive phrases. I do phrases based on the Word and find they come to life when I speak them out loud and tap on them. Allow yourself to believe it in your heart and ignore your head. Pretend, if you have to. The truth is that all of this is true. You can pretend/imagine the truth and it will literally change your brain cells.

Develop the habit of focusing on the truth.

IMAGINE THE TRUTH, while you tap on it.
Feel it.
Speak it.
Agree with it.

Below are some phrases to get you started:

I believe God is good and loves me.
I believe God is compassionate and wants me to be well.
I believe God has provided for my healing.
I believe Jesus died for my sins, so I could be free from the curse.
I believe sickness is part of the curse and I'm free from the curse, because Jesus became a curse for me, so I could be well.
I believe healing belongs to me legally.
I believe healing is God's will for me.
I believe God wants me well.
I believe God is greater than the enemy.
I believe I'm greater than the enemy, because greater is He that is in me than He that is in the world.
I believe all sickness is curable by God.
I believe all things are possible to the one who believes.
I believe God loves me as much as anyone else He has ever healed.
I believe sickness has no legal right to be in my body.

I believe that the Holy Spirit guides me into all the truth in the area of healing.
I believe I have authority over all the power of the enemy.
I believe God is love.
I believe God loves me just as I am.
I believe God forgives me.
I believe God is in me.
I believe God is all-powerful.
I believe in miracles.
I believe I can have a miracle.
I believe miracles are easy for God.
I believe I can be healed, even if I'm not perfect.
I believe satan cannot keep me sick.
I believe I am greater than _____ (Lyme, CFS, Fibro, diabetes, cancer, etc.)
I believe in Jesus.
I believe I have faith.
I believe I can have great faith.
I believe my faith is growing.
I believe my faith is enough.
Faith works by love; I walk in love, so I have faith.
I choose to walk in love.
I forgive all who have judged me.
I forgive all who have been unkind to me.
I forgive all who have failed me.
I forgive myself for not being perfect.
I choose to walk in love.
I choose to believe in love.
I choose the path of love.
I choose the way of love.
Love never fails; I walk in love, so I cannot fail.
Faith pleases God; I have faith, therefore, I please God.
I have faith and I please God.
Love covers all transgressions.
God is love.
God covers all my transgressions.
My sins are forgiven therefore healing belongs to me.
I choose to believe I have choices in my life.
I choose to believe I am heal-able.
I choose to believe I can be well.
I choose to believe I can have perfect health.
I choose to believe God is not withholding.

I choose to believe I have a legal right to be well.
I choose to believe I am not alone.
I choose to believe God forgives all my sins and heals all my diseases.
I want the habit of sickness (or Lyme or CFS or cancer or???) to be removed from my body and brain and emotions.
I choose to believe I am an extremely healthy, hearty person.
I choose to believe I can choose health.

Jesus said,

"The Kingdom of heaven suffers violence
and the violent take it by force."

Webster's definition of Violence: Vehement feeling or expression: FERVOR

FERVOR: Passion, marked by forceful energy, impassioned, fervid, deeply felt.

Jesus said,

"The violent take the Kingdom of God by force."

Donna's amplified version of that:

The impassioned exert forceful energy to seize, accept and completely possess the Kingdom of Heaven.

Don't let that statement get you into a place of striving. Let it inspire you. It's all about balance. Letting go and holding on, all at the same time. Ask God for wisdom to know when to hold on and when to let go. Each situation is different and needs to be walked out with the leading of the Holy Spirit.

NOTE: The chart of the following page includes the tapping points on the hand. I prefer to not do the gamut point or finger points. I find the shortened version found just before the Table of Contents works well for me. You might try both and see which you prefer.

EFT Tapping Points & Basic Instructions

1 The Setup

While massaging the tender point, repeat this phrase 3 times:

"Even though (insert issue here), I deeply and completely love and accept myself."

Ex: "*I'm afraid of spiders.*"

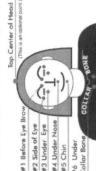
© 2010 Donna Crow

Tender Points

The tender points are located on the flat area of the upper chest. See white ovals in graphic above.

Notes: You can tap on the right or left side of your face and body.

When tapping on the Karate Chop points, use all four fingers of one hand to tap on the side of the other hand.

2 The Sequence

Reduce the setup phrase to the issue then state the issue once at each of the 12 points, while you tap on the point 5-7 times.

Ex: "*I'm afraid of spiders.*"

Use tip of finger to **tap**. Do not **pat** with flat of finger.

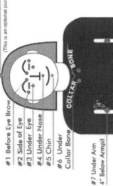

Top. Center of Head
(This is an optional point.)

#1 Before Eye Brow
#2 Side of Eye
#3 Under Eye
#4 Under Nose
#5 Chin
#6 Under Collar Bone
#7 Under Arm
4" Below Armpit

COLLAR BONE

© 2010 Donna Crow

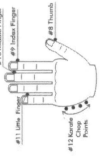

#10 Middle Finger
#9 Index Finger
#8 Thumb
#11 Little Finger
#12 Karate Chop Points

© 2010 Donna Crow

3 The Gamut

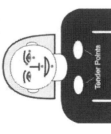

Gamut Point

© 2010 Donna Crow

Tap on the Gamut Point about 7 times for each action below:

1 Eyes closed
2 Eyes open
3 Eyes hard down to right
4 Eyes hard down to left
5 Rotating eyes full circle right
6 Rotating eyes full circle left
7 Humming any tune briefly
8 Counting from 1-5
9 Humming again briefly
(3-5 sec.)

4 Repeat The Sequence,

(Eye Brow to Karate Chop)

Congratulations, you have now completed one "round" of EFT. This whole process should not take more than two minutes.

For expert personal coaching go to: www.DonnaCrow.com.

Message Twenty-Three

Holiness

A few years back, I was walking across my bedroom, when suddenly the Presence of God filled me, and surrounded me. Specifically, He was revealing His Holiness to me and I involuntarily started saying, "Holy Jesus!" over and over. It was a profound, life-changing experience, yet, even while I was in the midst of this encounter with the God of all creation, I was thinking, "If anyone could hear me, they would think I had lost my mind." I kept thinking, "Holy Jesus, Batman." I swear, sometimes the flesh can be so irreverent.

I quickly got past my flesh and embraced what He was allowing me to feel. He let me experience His Holiness, and I realized that it is not what most people think. Holiness is not a world wary, sober attitude. It isn't about: cutting your hair,
> or not cutting your hair,
> or wearing closed-toe shoes,
> or not wearing makeup,
> or not wearing jewelry,
> or not playing cards,
> or not listening to music that has drums in it,
as some *holiness* churches teach. God's holiness is His complete and total freedom from the enemy.

Can you imagine what that would feel like? God has not one minute, minuscule, quark-sized, teeny tiny bit of darkness in Him. Not a speck! Darkness is from the enemy, and God has not one particle of the enemy in Him. The Word says, "God is light and in Him is no darkness at all." *That* is Holiness!

In my encounter with Him and His Holiness, I saw the absolute liberty and freedom of His purity. I understood that because the enemy has no place in God, God is totally free and is lighthearted and joyful. When He revealed His Holiness to me, this is what I experienced. I felt the lighthearted, joyful freedom that He feels, and it was beyond wonderful. Holiness is not morose self-control.

I repeat. Holiness is not some religious attempt at piousness, achieved by refraining from anything that might give your flesh pleasure. Nor is it the wearing of a veil, or the absence of makeup, or hiding your wrists for fear of arousing a man. No! It is absolute freedom and liberty from the enemy, and that is what God wants for us. He wants us to *be in the light as He is in the light*, and He wants us to be full of Joy.

The Word also says God is love. Not that He *has* love, *or is loving*, but that He *is* Love. He is pure love, and Light is what love looks like. When you walk in love, you increase the light in your life. You increase your own freedom from the enemy. You increase the holiness in your life, and it is a liberating, good thing, not some false religious constraint. When you walk in love, you connect with your spirit, and His Spirit, and the Life and Light of Christ flows in you.

So what is the point? Truth sets people free. The truth about God's Holiness increases our freedom. Lies about Holiness keep us from freedom. For me, the word Holiness had an icky connotation, inspiring pictures of cloistered Monks and cranky people burdened by the fear of enjoying life. It was lovely for God to let me experience His Holiness and be set free of that image forever. Holiness is freedom from sickness, from fear, from pain, from lies, from treachery, from loneliness, from anger, from misunderstanding, and from the enemy. Holiness is freedom! And God wants you to be Holy as He is Holy. He wants you to be full of joy because you are free. He has never wanted anything else for us but joyous freedom.

If you are born-again, you have the life and nature of Christ in your spirit. You can walk, more and more, out of that source every day. You can have more and more freedom from the enemy's influence. It's a matter of choice and practice. We can practice walking out of our spirit instead of being led by our senses. We can have more and more light, be more and more Holy and, therefore, increasingly free.

Every step you take toward Him and His truth is a step you take toward the light, and away from the darkness. It is a step toward freedom, and away from torment. The enemy would love for you to not believe he even exists, that way he can keep you in prison. Or, he would like you to engage in religion and works of the flesh, which are also torment. Don't let the enemy steal the beauty of Holiness from you. Don't let him make the word *Holy* a negative thing for you. Pursue Holiness by pursuing what Christ has purchased for you. He has transferred you from the kingdom of darkness to the Kingdom of Light. You can live out of either kingdom. It is your choice: your flesh, which is sense-ruled, or your spirit, which is full of light, power and freedom.

Holy people are free people.
Jesus came to give us life and that more abundantly.
Holiness is abundant life.
Holiness is freedom from sickness and poverty.
Holiness is freedom from the enemy.
Holiness is full of joy, unspeakable and full of Glory.

I'm eagerly seeking holiness.

Holiness

Message Twenty-Four

Summary

I thought I'd do a little recap of some of the things we have covered.

Jesus came not to do His own will, but that of the Father, Jehova-Rapha, the self-existent One Who reveals Himself as our healer/physician.

Jesus is the will of God, Jehova-Rapha, in action.

Jesus had compassion and healed ALL who came to Him.

Jesus commissioned all who believed in Him to heal the sick.

Jesus gave us authority over ALL the power of the enemy.

Jesus said,

ALL things are possible to the one who believes.

Healing is a thing that is possible to the one who believes.

Jesus said,

Whatever you desire when you pray, believe that you have received and you will.

Jesus carried our sin, sickness, disease, pain, and infirmities, so we could be righteous and healed.

Summary

We have the mind of Christ and we can live out of that rather than the mind of our flesh.

We are the righteousness of God in Christ Jesus.

All the promises of God are yes in Christ.

Healing is a promise, and it is yes in Christ.

If our heart does not condemn us, we can have whatever we ask for.

We walk in obedience; we walk in forgiveness; we walk in love, and it assures our heart before Him.

If we still are bound by condemnation, we can pray and ask the Lord to set us free from self-condemnation and the condemnation of the enemy.

We can also do EFT for lying emotions that conflict with our faith.

When we pray according to God's will, we know that He hears us, and if He hears us, we know we have the thing we have asked of Him.

We know healing is God's will for *all*. Jesus never refused healing to anyone.

> Jesus is the same yesterday, today, and forever.

> Jesus does not refuse healing to anyone today.

> Our faith takes what Jesus has purchased for us.

> Faith is the substance of things hoped for, the conviction that healing is ours, even if we can't see it instantly.

> Faith is the nature of our spirit.

> Faith pleases God.

> Faith works by love.

> Without faith, you cannot please God.

Faith is confidence in God's compassionate nature.

Faith is confidence in God's will.

Faith is confidence that we are redeemed from the curse.

Faith is confidence in truth.

Faith believes that Jesus attained our right to healing with His own shed blood.

Faith believes God wants us well.

Faith believes and receives.

Faith does not *perceive* and receive; it *believes* and receives.

Faith is confidence in God's revealed will.

Faith takes back what the enemy has stolen.

Faith lives in your spirit.

You can choose to have faith.

You can believe the Word of God.

You can be healed, and God will be glorified.

Summary

Message Twenty-Five

The Strength
Which God Supplies

*J*esus said, "Take My yoke upon you and learn from Me, for My burden is easy and My yoke is light." If you try to walk through life being spiritual in your own strength, then you might find life exhausting and difficult. If, however, you remember that Jesus is the living vine and you are only a branch, and that apart from Him you can do nothing, then you can rest and let Him do the heavy lifting.

You can say,

> "God, I have no idea how to get well, or understand your Word, or love my enemy, or forgive, or be wise, or be good, etc. I need You to do it for me."

I'm telling you that God loves that kind of prayer. Nothing good dwells in your flesh. You are the righteousness of God in Christ Jesus, but that is the reality of your spirit, not your flesh. You can, however, live from your spirit by dependence on God.

Colossians 2:6 says,

> "As you therefore have received Christ Jesus the Lord, so walk in Him."

What does that mean? Well, you received Christ by being totally helpless, right? Knowing that you could not save yourself, you asked Him to save you, and you accepted Him as your spiritual Savior. This is also how you walk with Him, with complete dependence on Him and His ability.

There is another verse that says, "Having begun in the Spirit, are you now being perfected in the flesh?" The answer to that question should be, "No!" However, multitudes of believers are trying to do exactly that. They are trying to use their flesh to fix their flesh. As a result, they are exhausted and disheartened. What we are supposed to do is become as a child and ask the Lord to enable us to live from our spirit, filled with the Holy Spirit. This is the place of freedom.

When you make an effort to be obedient, make sure you do it expecting God to supply the ability, the power, and the results. Otherwise, you are starting in the spirit and trying to be perfected in the flesh. The end result will be self-condemnation and discouragement.

I think I told this story here before, but maybe I didn't. I had a step-dad that was a pretty miserable human in some ways, lots of anger and unpleasantness. Years after he died, I had nightmares about him. Nothing bad was happening in the dream; I merely dreamed that he was alive, which, for me, was a nightmare, because he was such an angry, violent person. I woke up from one such dream and said to God, "Obviously I have not forgiven him, or I would not be dreaming about him. I have tried to forgive him, and I really thought I had, but the dream has shown me that I have not. So, if I have to forgive Him, You will have to do it because I cannot." I knew I couldn't do it anymore than I could turn into a bird and fly; so I prayed the prayer, felt nothing, and went on my way trusting it to the Lord.

I truly made it God's job to do what I could not. I was sincere and willing, but very much knew I was unable on my own to do this thing. I was also in faith; I was totally confident that He would give me the ability. About a month later I was walking across my living room, when I suddenly had a mini vision of him. It was an 8 x 10 glossy photo of a headshot of my step-dad and, when I saw it, I felt total love for him, like he was my best friend. Because I chose to humble myself, admit my inability, and trust God to do what I could not, He did it.

I do that with everything now. I refuse to try to do anything in my own strength. I give Him my willingness—to forgive or love or obey, etc.—

and He gives me His ability. And now I find that Jesus was correct; His burden is easy, and His yoke is light.

When I falsely *feel* like He has let me down, I go to Him and say, "I know this is the height of stupidity, but I *feel* like you have let me down. Please help me to not feel this way." And, delightfully, He lifts it right off of me.

The other option would be to try to not feel let down, or to try to love Him in my own strength. Don't try to love Him in your own strength. Don't try to obey in your own strength. Don't try to get your healing in your own strength. Don't try to walk in truth in your own strength. Be willing to walk in love, be willing to obey, be willing to be wise and to "get it," but be helpless to do it. Make all of it His job, and He will supply the ability. It is a place of freedom and lightheartedness and peace.

Jesus said,

> "Apart from Me you can do Nothing!"

Believe Him. Don't try to do life on your own.

> Jesus is God's will in action.

> He healed ALL who came to Him
> of ALL sickness and ALL disease.

If you don't get that, be willing to get it, and ask God to do what you can't, and enable you to get it—and He will.

Message Twenty-Six

What Is Actually Real?

*O*ur perception is that the world we view with our eyes is what is real, which means sickness seems more real to us than supernatural healing, which means that we stay sick. In order for us to connect with the power of God and receive healing, we will have to *look* beyond what our eyes see and *see* with our heart. Jesus talked about those who had eyes to see, but couldn't see, and ears to hear, but couldn't hear. In that parable, He implied that we could make a choice to *look beyond* what we see in the natural, and increase our freedom.

Paul, writing to the Corinthians, said, "We walk by faith and not by sight." When you walk by sight instead of faith, then you are (as Jesus said) one who has eyes, but cannot see. You can't see into Heaven with your natural eyes, but you can see into Heaven with your heart. You can believe the testimony of others who have gone before. You can act on what you *see* with your heart, and it can change what you see with your natural eyes.

Let's look at a few scriptures concerning this.

Hebrews 11:3 says:

> "By faith we understand that the worlds were prepared by the word of God, so that what is seen was not made out of things which are visible."

Colossians 1:15-16 says:

"And He is the image of the invisible God, the firstborn of all creation.

For by Him all things were created, both in the heavens and on earth, visible and invisible, whether thrones or dominions or rulers or authorities—all things have been created by Him and for Him

And He is before all things, and in Him all things hold together."

Isaiah 25:7 says:

"And on this mountain He will swallow up the covering which is over all peoples, even the veil which is stretched over all nations."

Basic Reality:

The world we see was made by faith, out of what we cannot see, by a God we cannot see. Right now, there is a world that exists beyond what is visible to us. It is called invisible, but in reality it is only invisible to us. To those who dwell in that world, it is as real and solid and visible as our natural world. Unfortunately, there is a veil between our visible reality and the realm that is invisible to us. That veil keeps us from enjoying a connection with God through our physical senses. By faith, however, we can connect with the unseen and it will change the seen. The invisible world can change the visible world, and that is what is necessary in order to receive a healing miracle.

The spiritual can change the natural.
The non-physical can change the physical.
The truth can change your facts,
because spiritual truth is greater than natural fact.

The natural fact may be that *I am terminally ill,* but the spiritual truth is that *Jesus bore my sickness and my pain and my disease,* and I don't have to remain sick.

Every time someone like me experiences the supernatural healing that Jesus purchased for us, it is because spiritual truth changed natural fact, but how? How do we get invisible truth to change the visible facts? By having faith in the invisible truth, rather than the visible facts, by praying and believing we receive healing, based on the invisible truth, rather than the visible facts. By exercising our spiritual authority and requiring/demanding that the healing Christ purchased for us manifest in our body. When you do that, *invisible truth* releases the power of God, which changes the *visible facts*.

There is a verse that says, "Resist the devil, and he will flee from you, draw near to God and He will draw near to you." (James 4:7) When you choose to believe the unseen, spiritual truth that Jesus already bore your pain and sickness, you are resisting the devil and drawing near to God, and He responds by drawing near to you.

From the invisible, He reaches toward you with power that changes your visible world. It is your faith in invisible truth that draws you near to God and activates His power toward you. The invisible God, in the invisible world, has got the goods. He has the healing, and He wants us to receive it, but we have to resist the visible and reach out to the invisible to get it.

Resist the visible
and embrace the invisible,
until it changes the visible.

Here again is some of the truth that can change your facts, *if* you believe you receive it:

Your sins are forgiven,

You are no longer under the curse,

Sickness is a part of the curse,

You are redeemed from the curse, and therefore from sickness,

All the promises of God are yes for you in Jesus,

Healing is a promise, which is "yes" for you in Jesus,

Healing is God's will,

Jesus came to do God's will and He healed ALL who came to Him, of
ALL diseases,

Jesus is the same yesterday and today and forever,
so He still heals all who come to Him.

Jesus became sin so you could be the righteousness of God.

Jesus became sick so you could be well.

Jesus said, "All things are possible to the one who believes."

His Holy Angels are mighty in strength
and perform the voice of His word.

We speak it, and they perform it.

We exercise authority by speaking His word, and they perform it.

We command the body to be healed, and they perform it.

The problem is that our visible world can be so *in our face* that all that
truth just seems unreal to us compared to how sick we feel, or how
much pain we are in—making it difficult to believe we receive. Does
that mean our situation is hopeless? No.

Remember this simple, powerful truth: *Resist the devil, and he will
flee from you, draw near to God and He will draw near to you.* That is
a guarantee. We *can* resist what we see and feel. We *can* resist the
lie that God doesn't want us to be healed. We *can* resist the feeling
that we don't deserve to be healed. We *can* resist the lie that God
doesn't love us, and Jesus is a fake, and that we will die sick. We *can*
resist the lies and draw near to God, and He will draw near to us.

You cannot reach toward God without Him reaching back. I guarantee
you that if you reach toward Him, He will reach toward you, and it will
change your world. If He was only a figment of people's imaginations,
then our efforts would be in vain, but He is not. He is real, and He is
eager to reveal Himself to us and comfort us and guide us.

Jesus said the Holy Spirit would guide us into all truth. He doesn't
force that guidance upon us, but when we acknowledge that *apart*

from Him we can do nothing, and we invite Him to teach us and guide us, He will.

We have a choice to walk by faith in the unseen, or be bound by what we can see and feel. We can take steps to look beyond the visible to the invisible, and be strengthened in our spirit. We can develop spiritual senses that make the unseen world more real to us than the seen. We can feed our spirit and see with eyes of faith, or we can feed the flesh and be bound by what we see and feel in the natural realm.

I know that some of you who are reading are so tired emotionally that you just don't feel like you can do much except survive each day, yielding to your flesh. Remember that *apart from Jesus you can do nothing.* Don't try to reach toward God in your own strength. Just tell Him you want to reach, but just don't have one tiny bit of ability to do so. Ask Him to help you reach toward Him. Ask Him to help you seek Him, and He will.

What Is Actually Real?

Message Twenty-Seven

The Challenge

*R*ecently, the Lord requested that I do a fast. Don't panic. I don't mean a no-food fast. I mean a personal version of a Daniel fast. If you read the book of Daniel, you will see that Daniel had a habit of fasting now and then. He didn't always do a total fast, where you don't eat any food; he did fasts where he just ate survival food, no treats. He combined this partial-food fast with increased prayer. Invariably, the result was that he received the answer he was seeking.

Recently, the Lord challenged me to do a similar fast. As a result of doing that fast, I have enjoyed more clarity, and have had some major breakthroughs in spiritual revelations that are propelling me forward. So, I was thinking about this group, and it seems to me that there is enough information in what I have shared for anyone listening to be healed IF the teaching penetrates their heart. Because fasting can help with that process, I would like to encourage/challenge you to do a Daniel fast.

A Daniel fast helps you to disconnect from the onslaught of natural-realm facts and help you connect with spiritual realm truth. It is a practical way to help you take steps to get what legally belongs to you. It helps you to connect with spiritual truth that can change your natural facts.

Remember that the Word says,

"Faith comes by hearing and hearing by the Word of God."

Faith doesn't come
by watching secular television.
It doesn't come by reading novels.

It doesn't come by complaining about the government.
It doesn't come by reading the newspaper.
It doesn't come by worrying.
It doesn't come by feeling sorry for ourselves.
It doesn't come by studying nutrition.
It doesn't come by building model airplanes.

Faith comes by hearing the Word of God, so spending time in the Word is recommended, and that includes literature based on the Word also.

Part of the fast that I did was to avoid television, conversations that were useless, and distractions that did nothing but entertain. I fasted from the onslaught of the world.

No newspapers,
No magazines,
No TV,
No radio,
No secular music,
No studying health on the Internet.

What?! Smile.

Yes, I took a break from the study of natural healing. For those who spend long hours on the net doing health research, this can seem like a torturous thought.

You can make your own list. Maybe: no crossword puzzles, no knitting, no bowling???

It can be anything that you use to entertain or distract yourself.

I also fasted from fun foods.

No "once a week" muffin from the co-op,
Nothing to drink except water,
No tea unless it is medicinal and needed,
No flavored drinks, just plain water,
No snacks,
No entertainment food, just meat, vegetables, fruit, nuts, and legumes for survival.

No coffee, unless you are addicted and can't quit cold turkey.

(This fast is not about quitting coffee; it is about no "entertainment food." I have coffee once every few weeks. If I were hooked on coffee, I would not have tried to stop coffee as that was not the point of my fast. It was about reducing my focus on the natural and amping up my focus on God. If I had tried to quit a coffee addiction, I would have been extremely focused on my body, and it would have been counter-productive for me. Perhaps you don't feel that way. I suggest you ask Him to help you set the parameters of your personal fast.)

During my personal fast, I did do computer work that I had to do, but I avoided any work that I didn't have to do. If I felt a check in my spirit about pursuing something on the Net, I took heed and avoided it.

When we do a fast like this, we are resisting the hold that our senses have on us. We begin to become more sensitive in the spirit, and God draws near to us. It is extremely beneficial in helping us to believe God, rather than being sense-ruled. Daniel did this type of fast for extended periods, in an effort to break through and take ground spiritually, and it never failed him. I assure you, if you do a similar fast, you will be drawing near to God, and He will draw near to you. You will come out the other side stronger, and you might come out healed.

In addition to fasting from foods and activities that strengthen the flesh, it is a time to practice things that strengthen the spirit.

Here are some recommendations:

Spend time in the Word reading and declaring (out loud) scriptures that say God wants you well. I recommend getting a three-ring notebook and writing down scriptures and thanking God that they are true regarding you—daily.

Jesus said, "Blessed are those who have not seen and yet have believed." When you do this fast and confess the Word over yourself, you will begin to be a person who is blessed, because they believe what they cannot see. The Word of God is alive and full of power, and when you speak it with faith, it has an effect in the spirit realm and begins to change your world.

Repeatedly declare things like, "Jesus became sin so I could be the righteousness of God" and "Jesus became sick so I could be healed." "Jesus redeemed me from the curse of the law, which is sickness, and therefore sickness is illegal for me."

You can tap on your acupressure points when you do this, and it will penetrate your heart more. I declare all kinds of healing scriptures and tap while doing it. It is wonderful. That way, you hit it from both the natural and supernatural realm.

Spend some time each day being thankful and praising God. You are drawing near to Him when you do that, and He will make Himself known to you.

Do a little EFT daily for various emotions that you have that you know are not truth:

I'm afraid I'll never get well
I'm afraid everyone else will get it except me
I feel like God doesn't like/love me
I feel sorry for myself

In previous messages, I did more extensive lists. You could use these to get started and let God lead you. He knows the lies you have in your emotions. Invite Him to help you eliminate them one by one.

You can also pray for others during this time and make declarations over them.

Examples:

I thank You that _____'s sins are forgiven.

I thank You; Father, that _____ is redeemed from the curse, and sickness has no legal right to stay in their body.

I thank You that Jesus became sin so _____ could be the righteousness of God in Christ Jesus.

I thank You that Jesus became sick so that _____ could be well.

I thank You that You are Jehova-Rapha, the Lord that heals
_____.

I thank You that all the promises are yes for
_____.

I thank You that there is now no condemnation for
_____.

I thank You for a spirit of wisdom and revelation in the true knowledge of God for _____.

You get the idea. Any scripture that supports your faith can be turned into a prayer of thanksgiving for yourself or someone else.

Also, during your fast you might want to read literature that supports your goal; one that I just read and found superior is *Christ the Healer,* by F.F. Bosworth. It is jam-packed with evidence that supports your legal position, and I highly recommend it. There may be other good books out there on healing, but I seriously doubt if there is a better one. Hundreds of thousands have been healed by reading it and acting on what it teaches.

Yesterday evening, after I had written the previous three posts, I went to watch some Christian television. What was being shared was a wonderful confirmation of what I had written. The speaker told of being given a diagnosis of incurable illness. His first response was similar to what anyone's would be, but he soon went into violence mode. Remember that Jesus said, "The Kingdom of heaven suffers violence, and the violent take it by force." This person violently attacked this issue with spiritual weapons. He locked himself in his bedroom and saturated himself with healing scriptures, and scriptures that declare that God is compassionate and loves us. He listened to tapes while he slept. 24 hours a day he saturated himself with the Word—planting the incorruptible seed of the Word in his heart and speaking it out of his mouth. Five days later he exited his prayer chamber, calling out to his wife, saying, "I've got it." He went to his doctor and told his doctor he was healed. His doctor did an exam and confirmed that he was healed.

Another man shared that he had, had a back problem. He had one ruptured disk, and others were out of place. He said his lower spine was a mess. He chose the same path as the man did in the previous story, and within three days he knew he had won in the spirit. He continued to confess the Word over himself, and 18 months later, he went for another MRI to see how his back was looking, and was told it was totally healed. The ruptured disk was now perfect and in place, and all his vertebrae and disks were perfect and in place. He may have been healed much sooner, as he was out of pain much sooner, but he didn't get tested right away. I'm not sure why he waited so long for the MRI—probably because he is extremely busy ministering.

Both of these people took themselves out of everyday life and took steps to connect with the truth that changes the facts, and they both got what God says is ours: healing.

This really works folks. God is alive and well, and healing those who believe, and anyone *can* believe. Healing belongs to all of us.

God loves you, just like He loves Jesus.

He is not withholding.

You are forgiven and loved,

and healing belongs to you.

Message Twenty-eight

The Key:
Believing You Receive

I talked about this before, but I want to cover it again and make sure it is clear because believing you receive is the key that makes everything we discussed come together. It is the catalyst.

Once you have read the Word and have understood that healing belongs to you, that healing is God's will, and you have a legal right to healing, what do you do next? How do you experience healing?

I spent 18 years certain that healing belonged to me, but it did not produce healing in my body because I failed to believe I received. I kept saying, *God is going to heal me.* I kept putting it out there in the future. Believing you receive *now* is the key that turns the ignition and fires the engine. You can have all the parts of the engine, but if you don't turn the key, there will be no ignition. In this case, believing you *have* received is the key.

Remember, I spoke earlier about "believing you receive," instead of "perceiving you receive."

In Mark 11:23-24, Jesus said,

> "Truly I say to you, whoever says to this mountain, 'Be taken up and cast into the sea,' and does not doubt in his heart, but believes that what he says is going to happen, it shall be granted him.

"Therefore I say to you, all things for which you pray and ask, believe that you have received them, and they shall be granted you."

That is the key.

Believing you receive, BEFORE you see it,

Instead of "perceiving you receive," based on a lack of symptoms.

Believing is based on what the Word says, which is that Christ redeemed us from the curse, and sickness has no right to be in your body. It is Biblically correct to believe that when you command sickness to go, and command your body to be healed in the name of Jesus that it is done. Not that it is going to be done, but that it is done.

Based on the fact that God, Who is your healer, is compassionate and wants you well.

Based on: "It's not about you being perfect, but you being forgiven."

Based on: "all the promises are yes in Jesus,"
and healing is a promise and, therefore, healing is yes in Jesus.

Based on: Christ bore your pain and sickness, and you don't have to.

Based on: He forgives all our sins and heals all our diseases.

Based on: He is the God Who heals us.

Based on: Christ has redeemed us from the curse of the Law, part of which is sickness.

Based on: Spiritual law rather than symptoms.

It is having faith in the character and nature of God and our legal standing in Christ. Believing that, He is not a liar, and if He said He is our healer, He is our healer. It is believing in the character and nature of Jesus, Who was moved with compassion and healed *all* who came to Him, of *all* diseases. It is believing that the work Jesus did on the cross is enough and that you don't have to work your way to healing.

166

All you have to do is believe that He bore your sins and your sickness, so you don't have to bear them.

Nothing is lacking in Christ's redemptive work. You cannot redeem yourself; you can only humble yourself and accept that Jesus purchased your freedom for you. Jesus suffered for you so that you could be free. You don't have to suffer to be free. All you have to do is believe in what He did for you, and it has to be present tense.

By saying, *I believe Jesus is going to heal me,* you make it future tense, and your healing will always be out there in the future. When you command sickness to go, and command your body to be well, and know in your heart that, "Jesus bore my pain and sickness and, therefore, I believe I am healed," and don't doubt (even if you still have symptoms), then your faith is present tense and you *will* have the thing you believe you have. But it is a heart belief, not a head belief. Mental assent doesn't get the job done. In fact, your head can doubt, and your heart can still believe and receive.

As Jesus said, "it shall be granted to you." Well, the truth is that the word "granted" was not in the original. The translators put it in, in an effort to help it make sense to English speakers, but it actually says, ". . . it shall be to you."

Remember the woman with the issue of blood? She made her way through the crowd to Jesus and touched His garment and power went out of Him, and she felt in her body that she was healed? Well, it is fascinating to me that Jesus asked, "Who touched my clothes?" He perceived that power had gone out of Him, but He did not know who it went out to. She made a draw on the power in Jesus, and she was healed, even though He didn't know who had touched Him. When He asked who had touched Him, she revealed herself, and then He said to her that her faith had healed her.

She didn't go to Jesus and ask for healing, whereupon Jesus checked her out, decided she was worthy to be healed, and then healed her. No. She said to herself, "If I just touch the hem of His garment I will be made well," and what she said and believed, she received.

Jesus, by His sacrifice, has provided power to heal you. When your faith makes a draw on that power, it goes out. It is not about Jesus picking and choosing who is granted healing, based on judging their character. It is an automatic system that He has already set in motion, and when you believe, you receive, "It shall be to you." It might be by an Angel who touches you. It might be because an evil spirit leaves you. It might be by the Holy Spirit inside you. How it works, I don't know, but I do know that it works. And this is true with all the promises of God, not just healing. "Whatsoever things you desire when you pray, believe that you have them, and they shall be (granted) to you. "

If you pray and wait to see what happens, in order to determine if you *got it* or not, then you are not *believing you receive.* This is how I missed it for days, weeks, months and years on end. When you can stand on the Word, and believe what it says about you, rather than believing what your symptoms say about you, then you will have it. This is not something you do with your flesh. It has to be a single-minded, heart action. You fill your heart with the Word on healing, and then let it come out of your mouth, declaring that it is yours. *Now!* Believing that the Lord is *going* to heal you is not it. Believing that you have prayed according to His will and that He has heard you, and that you have what you have asked for *now*—while you still have symptoms—that is the key. (1 John 5:14-15) In my experience, the symptoms leave rather quickly when I do this.

Last night, after I had written the preceding, I was reading a book called *Understanding The Anointing* by Kenneth Hagin. It's a great little book, and something I read in it confirmed the above. He said he saw more people healed of cancer than anything else, but it was almost never instantaneous. The healing would start when he prayed for people, but it would not be complete for eight to thirteen days, and sometimes a few days longer. He taught people to believe they received, in spite of their symptoms. As a result, they held on to that, and resisted their symptoms, and many were healed.

I repeat. This is where I missed it. I would pray, and when my symptoms didn't immediately abate, I would assume that God didn't grant me the thing I had asked, which led to confusion, because the Word says He will grant us the thing we ask for. I kept missing the truth that Jesus also said to believe you HAVE received it and you shall.

You can't believe AFTER you have received. You have to believe BEFORE you receive. The only way you can do that is to stand on your legal position and trust in the nature of God, that He is compassionate and wants you well. You have to focus on the truth, rather than the facts. It is not an emotional belief; it is a simple confidence in what the Word says is true.

It's not enough to believe that God is your healer. You have to believe that, when you exercise your authority over the enemy and sickness (based on the finished work of Jesus), you are praying according to His will, and that He has heard you, and you have the thing you have asked/commanded and are, therefore, healed.

Making the truth present tense is a key.

Believing you *have* received
before you see the answer is a key.

I have been purposely repetitive here because I want you to get this. I missed it for a *long* time all the while thinking that God was withholding. I don't want you to go through that. I want you to get it quickly, so I have tried to repeat it until it is clear. That being said, don't try to get this in your own strength. Ask the Lord to help you to believe you have received, and He will.

Final Thought

I believe God wants you to be well, *now*. It took me quite some time to get healed, not because He was withholding, but because I lacked understanding and was not well enough to reach out for help from other people. I had to work toward breakthrough on my own, in my own home. Many of those who are reading are in that position, and I hope you will be helped by what I have said.

The bottom line for me is that the Holy Spirit knows the specific way out for *you*. Remember to let the Holy Spirit do the heavy lifting, i.e., enabling you in every way. That is what Grace is; God's ability flowing through our faith-filled weakness. It is like a parent who holds onto the bicycle, while their child rides their bike or supports them while they "float" in the swimming pool. You make your small effort, and God makes it work.

If these pages have helped you in any way, I would love to hear from you. Or, if you have questions, you can write me here: deardonnacrow@gmail.com

Other Donna Crow Publications:

Enjoy Your Rights & Privileges Now

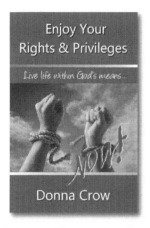

Rights & Privileges is a compilation of the fundamental rights and privileges of the Born-again believer in Christ. It is a crash course in the abundant life Christ said He came to give us. Find out if you have been living beneath your inheritance in Christ. Do you know that you can live a supernatural life and enjoy living within God's means, rather than limiting yourself to your own natural ability to enjoy life, live well, and do good.

Do you know that God has made hundreds of promises to us and is anxious to honor His promises?

Do you know what those promises are?
Do you know what your rights and privileges are?
Do you know how to live within God's means?

Enjoy Your Rights & Privileges Now . . . Living Within God's Means, documents most, if not all, the promises of God to us, and clearly states what our rights and privileges are. Why? Because knowing what belongs to you is the first step to enjoying what belongs to you.

Do you know what a promise is? It is a declaration that you absolutely will do something, or give something, or provide something. It is a guarantee that you will do what you say you will do.

Okay, so . . . God, aka Yahweh the Creator of the Universe, has made some promises from which He promises He will not turn back, i.e., renege. In other words, God has made many promises and, in addition, He has promised that He will not revoke, or renege, or change His mind, or fail to keep His promises. He has made hundreds of promises and then promised to keep His promises.

So let's talk about His promises for a moment. God's promises are all supernatural. They are good and great things, even remarkably wondrous things that you can have by His power, which you cannot have by your own power. Sound interesting? It does to me.

I realize then, that I can either walk through life trying to succeed and enjoy my life based on my own limited potential and abilities, or I can hook into His supernatural ability and live within His means. .

Foundational, of course, would be to know what belongs to me. What has He actually promised, or even inferred, that I can have. Faith is a major factor in living within God's means, and Faith is always based on knowing what belongs to us. Paul said, Faith comes by hearing, and hearing by the word of God. Pretty simple, really. Knowing the truth is foundational to having faith in truth, and having faith in truth is foundational to enjoying the benefits of that truth.

Believing is foundational to receiving.
Knowing is foundational to believing.

There are services available today to help people find inheritances that they didn't even know existed, with a view to helping them lay claim to what belongs to them. Banks, businesses, government agencies and other entities across the nation are believed to be holding at least ten Billion in unclaimed assets, belonging to an estimated 30 Million American's who have no idea they have an inheritance or an asset waiting for them to claim it.

I recently read one story of a homeless man from Bolivia, Thomas Martinez, who ran from the police when they tried to contact him to tell him he had inherited 6 million dollars. He has never been found.

So here is the big question: Do you know what belongs to you? Are you forfeiting your rights and privileges through lack of knowledge?

Enjoy Heaven Now

This is a book about one believer's delightful and personal experience of discovering the Father's desire to lavishly fellowship with all His children.

It is about extravagant worship and is intended to lead believers into a sustainable and liberating intimacy with the Lord.

Does God seem far away? You can change that. Learn how to draw near to Him, so that He draws near to you. Learn how to tap into Heaven's resources and *Enjoy Heaven Now.*

Smart Prayers

Prayers GOD Loves to Answer

DONNA CROW

FREE DOWNLOAD

Smart Prayers are prayers that God delights to answer.

They activate the Grace of God, releasing divine power, which enables us to live supernatural lives based on the resources of Heaven rather than our limited natural resources. I pray Smart Prayers daily, and always receive the help I have asked for. I have never had a "no" answer to a Smart Prayer . . . not even once.

My own experience with Smart Prayers started more than 30 years ago. I was watching a Christian television program where a young woman was sharing about difficult life circumstances she had experienced. She spoke about how she prayed and how God answered her prayer, and brought her through to victory.

When I heard her story, which I cannot now remember, I marveled at the prayer she prayed, which I also cannot now remember. What I do clearly remember is that I envied her for having the wisdom to pray such a profoundly Smart Prayer. I also remember feeling very inferior to her, and wishing that I were smart enough to pray those types of prayers . . . the ones that God loves to answer, the ones that activate miraculous interventions, personal transformation, increased freedom, absence of care, lightness of heart and more.

Then, in the midst of my personal disappointment with myself, I suddenly came alive! With great delight, it dawned on me that a really Smart Prayer would be to ask the Father to help me to pray Smart Prayers. How brilliant! So I did!

I prayed with complete confidence that He would answer that prayer. As I prayed, I pictured my life, stretching out before me, and imagined Him touching me from time to time throughout my life, inspiring me to pray Smart Prayers. Looking back over my life, I can clearly see that He has done just that. Since that original Smart Prayer, He has regularly given me wisdom to pray prayers that enable Him to move in my life with His power and provision. I have prayed in ways that, prior to that time, had never occurred to me.

I have also come to understand that He can help me with everything, not just the big stuff. As a result, I pray Smart Prayers daily and enjoy continuous divine enablement, whether I'm trying to figure out a computer program, or the best way to plant my garden, or how to help someone receive miraculous healing, or commanding bad weather to cease, etc. I have become hyper-conscious of the limitations of my body and soul to enable me to live a life of freedom or power. I have also become hyper-conscious of the fact that God is always available and wants to supernaturally supply me, every second of my life; and if I ask in faith I will receive, without fail.

Every human breath, every thought, every emotion and action can be filled with God's life, or it can be fueled by natural human effort. When we were born again, we were transferred from the kingdom of darkness to the Kingdom of Light. We now have access to Grace for every moment of our life. Smart Prayers activate His Grace and enable us to access and enjoy the supernatural resources of the Kingdom of Light. It's all about Grace. Grace enables us to live out of the Kingdom of Light now, and Smart Prayers activate Grace.

Type the link below into your browser to get your free copy:
http://donnacrow.com/SmartPrayers.html

Go to http://www.donnacrow.com
For other free Donna Crow publications.

Donna Crow is President and Founder of Fountain of Life Healing School, a non-profit where she teaches healing based on natural methods, as well as supernatural healing through prayer. She also has guest speakers from around the world who share their wealth of knowledge with listeners.

Classes are archived on the Internet here:

http://www.blogtalkradio.com/donna-crow

All classes are free, and open to the public.

You can also find Donna on the net at:

http://www.fol-hs.com
http://www.donnacrow.com

Thanks for reading!

If this book has touched your life,
and you'd like to share, please write:

deardonnacrow@gmail.com

Made in the USA
San Bernardino, CA
19 May 2017